The Passage

A NEW BEGINNING

The Passage

A NEW BEGINNING

April Love

ARPress
45 Dan Road Suite 5
Canton MA 02021

Hotline: 1(888) 821-0229
Fax: 1(508) 545-7580

Ordering Information:
Quantity sales. Special discounts are available on quantity purchases by corporations, associations, and others. For details, contact the publisher at the address above.

Printed in the United States of America.
ISBN-13:   Softcover   979-8-89356-958-2
                eBook   979-8-89356-959-9

Library of Congress Control Number: 2024909800

TABLE OF CONTENTS

The Passage Part I

The Passage Part II

The Passage Part I

CHAPTER I

Kelly awoke startled and sat up in bed. She then lay back down and thought about her dream. She could still visualize her grandmother Birdie sitting in a chair. She was trying to tell her something. She was waving her arms and pointing up in the air. Her eyes were red and wild looking and wide open with fear. Her mouth was moving but Kelly couldn't understand what she was saying. The only thing she was certain of was that she was trying to tell her something about her grandfather. Kelly closed her eyes and lingered for a moment in contemplation. This type of dream was pretty common place for her. As far back as she could remember she had experienced what she had determined were psychic premonitions in her dreams. These were dreams she would have about a person or an event that would usually come to pass. Many times instead of in a dream, she would suddenly find herself thinking of someone or an event that would later materialize.

At times it became an analyzing process for her as she would try to relive a dream to examine it more clearly to understand why she had experienced that particular dream. It was as though the minds or thoughts of others were somehow in contact with her mind, tumbling on a collision course reaching out for a place to be, to exist and she was there as a receiver; like a lonely space station designed to pickup these transmitted thoughts and events that were to come. She would try to understand her thinking process and why she seemed to be compelled to foresee these things that would unfold right before her eyes but she had never been able to grasped and understand why the premonitions kept coming. It seemed her mind never rested. She had wished many times that the seemingly endless train of thoughts would just suddenly stop and go away forever.

As she grew older if a dream or thought seemed to be a foreboding one she would sometimes feel apprehensive and fearful knowing her premonition might be about to occur. The apprehension and feeling of dread that would come over her would be followed by a whopping migraine that might last for hours or even days. As she lay in bed with her eyes closed her stomach began to feel queasy as she still contemplated the dream about her grandmother. She wanted to brush off the uneasy feeling as the hidden meaning began to grip her entire being. Then from out her bedroom window she heard a bird singing. She suddenly opened her eyes, jumped quickly out of bed and began gathering up a pile of clothes from the floor to take downstairs to wash.

"This is going to be the best summer ever" she thought. She had just graduated from high school and had made plans for that coming weekend to go to Panama City Florida with two of her classmates Linda and Regina. Linda's parents owned a condo there that they had bought for family getaways, although they rented it out most of the summer. They were going to take the girls down and would chaperone them for the weekend. That one summer vacation weekend was all Kelly and her friends had talked about for months and they were ecstatic about going.

Kelly ran downstairs with her arms full of clothes. Her long brown pony tail swished back and forth as she prissed passed her mother who was talking to someone on the phone. She threw her cloths in the washer and was headed back down the hall when she glanced into the kitchen. Her mother was standing very still facing the wall. She had her head down and was holding the phone receiver with both hands. Kelly came towards her and said

"Hey, Mom?" Her mother turned to face her. Her eyes were full of tears. As she spoke her voice quivered. "That was grandmother Birdie she said. Granddaddy died this morning, the paramedics said, they think of a heart attack. I just can't believe it, it was so sudden." Kelly rushed to her side and put her arms around her. She thought about her dream and how grandmother Birdie was trying to tell her something. Her mother sobbed, "Birdie said Albert didn't answer at the office. I'll try him again on his cell. Oh, how I dread giving him the news about Granddaddy."

After Kelly's mother broke the news to her father, he drove immediately to Birmingham to comfort his mother and to take care of his father's funeral arrangements. The next morning was Saturday, the day Kelly was to have left for the beach for that long anticipated weekend. Kelly's mother called to her from downstairs and asked if she had packed her clothes for the funeral. Kelly opened her small overnight bag she had packed to take to Florida. She took out her new beach towel, her new red two-piece bathing suit, tanning oil and flip flops. Sighing she replaced them with a sundress and her sling-back pumps for the funeral. They packed the car and as they started out the door Kelly grabbed the mail from the porch mailbox and began flipping through it and pulled out a letter addressed to her before handing the rest to her mother. Her heart sank. The letter was from Westwood College. She took a deep breath and opened it. It was an acceptance letter with an enrollment application.

She told her mother the good news in the car and pulled out the letter and read it aloud to share the news with her. Her mother smiled sweetly and said that was wonderful and how proud she was of Kelly. She said "You know how glad your father and I am that you decided to pursue a business degree." Her mother and father were both certified accountants, not to mention both were also real estate agents and owned their own business in Atlanta. Kelly just smiled at her mother's reply and didn't say much else because she knew at the time her mother had a lot on her mind. Kelly held the letter for a long time during the drive before putting it in her purse. She day dreamed most of the way to Birmingham. She visualized how college life would be and couldn't wait to see the campus again.

Her plans were that after buying her books she would buy new clothes. Regina and Linda had also applied to Westwood. Regina had been accepted but they hadn't heard from Linda. The three of them had talked about living together either on campus or maybe renting an apartment close by. This is so great she thought. Maybe I will finally meet some really great guy at the school. Kelly was eighteen and like any girl her age, she had boys on the brain. She was an old fashioned girl in her heart. She had her future somewhat planned out in her mind the way she thought her future should be. She had always dreamed that she would go to college and while in college or afterwards, it didn't matter, she would meet the perfect guy, her eternal soul mate, meant only for her. They would get married, buy a beautiful home, and have two kids, a dog and a cat. She could close her eyes and visualize the beautiful antebellum home they would live in, with a white picket fence and the whole nine yards. Yes, one day she would have a perfect life.

CHAPTER 2

The death of Kelly's grandfather had come as a shock to everyone. In their deep despair her father and grandmother made funeral arrangements for the following Monday. Kelly's grandfather, Albert Lewis Brown had many friends and he was thought of by all who had known him as a highly respected business entrepreneur and quite a character. He had made most of his business associates and friends through years for making business contacts. There were many of his friends and colleagues who respected and admired him for his life time of achievement in the real estate business and also for his contributions and involvement in his church. An article written in the paper said his reputation preceded him with each business endeavor he undertook. Through the years he had the reputation as a trusted business man and had established a good deal of wealth from real estate investments. It seemed the one factor that was always mentioned when his name was brought up was that he had a happy go lucky attitude towards life. He was born with the insides of a hard core salesman just like his father, Albert Brown Sr., Kelly's great grandfather who was said to have also known just inherently how to wheel and deal to become successful.

Kelly loved her grandfather and thought of him as a jolly man with a big heart. He was always smiling and would many times surprise her with little gifts when he came to visit their home. Kelly's father boasted that his father and grandfather were both hard working self-made men. They had gone through the depression when money was tight and you could bet on it that he could get blood out of a turnip. Her grandfather had owned Brown Real Estate Company in Birmingham for over thirty years. He and his partner William Norris formed their partnership in 1954. They named the company Brown Real Estate since the company was actually Albert Sr.'s brain child. The foundation of the company was funded from a portion of Albert Sr.'s early stock market investments that he willed to Kelly's grandfather.

Albert and his father had always had a tight bond and Albert idolized him. Kelly's father had begun his career in real estate by working in his father's office doing small errands as early as grammar school. When he was ten years old his mother was in a car accident and a month later died from a blood clot on her brain. His father remarried four years later to his stepmother Beatrice Bird who he loving called Mama Birdie. They never had children so he grew up as an only child thus; Albert spent a lot of time learning the ropes of his father's business. By the time he graduated from high school he was following right along in his father's footsteps knowing he wanted to sell real estate. He later decided to obtain a decree in accounting and worked for a few years for a small CPA firm. A few years later he got his real estate license and went to work full time with his father as Sales Manager.

Kelly's dad met Kelly's mother one weekend while attending a college buddy's birthday party who was living in Atlanta. Her mother was from Atlanta and after their marriage she insisted they live in Atlanta so she could be close to her mother and sister. Kelly had always sensed her father had been the happiest when he was working alongside his dad and that he hadn't wanted to uproot and move to Atlanta but had wanted to keep the peace with Kelly's mom and not have to move her from her home and family. It was around that time when her parents were newly married that Mr. Norris's son who owned a real estate business in Atlanta offered Kelly's father a position with his company. Albert informed his father he would be moving to Atlanta, but promised him he would work out of both offices and continue to be manager over sales in the Birmingham office. After awhile he got into the routine of commuting back and forth from Atlanta to Birmingham. After a few years Mr. Norris's son decided to sell his business and Kelly's father bought it. Kelly was born two years after her parents moved to Atlanta, so Atlanta had always been her home.

CHAPTER 3

About two weeks after the funeral, Kelly overheard her parents talking about her grandfather's business. Grandmother Birdie had closed the office the day of her Granddaddy's death and it hadn't been opened for at least two weeks. Her father said he was going to Birmingham the next day to meet with Grandmother Birdie and the family attorney to discuss his father's Will and other business matters. Grandmother Birdie and the attorney had been discussing her business options. The attorney had suggested she could hire someone to manage the business and if that didn't work out she could eventually sell it since Albert had his own business in Atlanta. Grandmother Birdie told Albert about the attorney's suggestion and that she didn't like the idea of a stranger managing their business. Albert tried to reassure her that all she needed was a good office manager and that he would make sure they hired the right person for the job. He said he would continue to drive down on a weekly basis as always and continue to be the Sales Manager.

Mama Birdie seemed too bewildered and stressed out to agree with her son about new management. She began to cry and told Albert she was afraid of what was going to happen to her without his father. She told him she didn't know if she could trust anyone other than him to run the business and that she would just as soon sell it. Albert told her he didn't want her to sell his father's business. She said she was squeamish about making financial decisions and that the business just confused her and that she

8

didn't want to deal with any of the problems. Albert tried to reassure her that he would make the right decisions regarding the business and ended their conversation by telling her not to worry and that he would take care of everything. He also spoke to their attorney and clarified before concluding their meeting that he understood his mother's concerns but that he was the executor of his fathers' estate and he would take care of all present and future business decisions with his mother's approval. He told their attorney he would be in touch with him in a few days and that he had to discuss the matter with Kelly's mother.

Kelly's grandfather had become quite successful during the last ten years. A large part of that success in the latter years was due to his real estate sales force that had been managed and run successfully by Kelly's father. Through the years Kelly's dad had devoted a great deal of his time and energy into his dad's business, maybe even more than his own business. The business he bought from Mr. Norris's son was much smaller than his father's and their company consisted of three realtor agents, Kelly's mother and himself. He knew that without the continued sales he would acquire from this father's business he wouldn't be able to continue to provide his family with what he would consider to be a sufficient income. Albert as the executor of his father's estate had not foreseen that one day he would be faced with the decision he was about to have to make. That evening after returning from Birmingham, he spoke to Kelly and her mother. He said he had decided it would be necessary for him to take over his father's business and that they would need to move to Birmingham. He let them know that Grandmother Birdie was very distraught over his father's death and he didn't feel she was really capable of making clear decisions about the business and had been talking to the attorney about selling it. He told Kelly's mother, "You know I would never agree to sell my father's business." He said even if he found a capable manager to run the office and his mother agreed to give it a shot, she still might decide to sell the business on down the road without even consulting him first. He said under the circumstances he had to do what he thought was best for everyone and that they would need to start looking for a house in Birmingham right away. He added that he hoped it wouldn't come to it but eventually he might have to close the Atlanta office, but until they were settled in the Birmingham office he would continue to commute back and forth between locations as usual.

Kelly saw her mother's expression of disappointment as her father unfolded his plans. He said since time is money, he wanted them to start making plans on moving right away and that they needed to get settled in Birmingham if possible by the end of the summer. He looked at her mother and said, "I'm sorry Kathy, but this is for the survival of my father's business, my mother's well being and our future. If I don't take over the business now, mother might try to sell it, and you know right now we rely on sales from both locations to meet overhead and right now we are in jeopardy of not meeting overhead. I've got to do what I've got to do." Kelly's mother put her arms around his shoulders gave him a hug and replied as she tried to hold back her tears that she only hoped he was going to breakdown and hire some extra office help in Birmingham because she couldn't handle that big office by herself. She then laughed and wiped the tears from her eyes. Her mother was also concerned about her own mother's well being. They had lived near Kelly's grandmother Evelyn all Kelly's life.

Her grandmother Evelyn had been a widower since Kelly was a baby. Her grandfather Pete was killed in an accident at the plant where he worked. While Kelly could barely remember him she grew up hearing about him a lot from her grandmother Evelyn. Kelly's mother believed she needed to protect her mom and lookout for her since her mom had no one else she could depend on except Kelly's mother. Grandmother Evelyn had also developed some health problems. Albert suggested that grandmother Evelyn and Kelly's Aunt Ellen could both move in with them temporarily after they find a house in Birmingham and then afterwards they could find a place of their own that would be close to them. Kelly realized her father felt he was doing the only thing he could do by moving back home and taking control of his father's business. He was doing what came natural to him to survive, to support his family and he seemed sure his father would have wanted it that way. Kelly was glad that her father was going to be able to move back to his hometown. She had always felt like he missed living in Birmingham. She could also sense a little of the mental anguish he was going through at the time and she felt sorry for him because he was finally going to be able to move back to his hometown but only because of the loss of this father.

CHAPTER 4

Had Kelly's parents considered her future? Atlanta had always been her home. She would have to move from a town where she grew up and the only town she had ever lived in. She would be leaving so many memories behind, so many places she enjoyed going to, not to mention her two best friends. She realized her plans to start college would be put on hold for the time being. She had missed her chance to go to Panama City that summer and she knew with the move coming up another opportunity for a vacation with Regina and Linda might be a long time coming if at all. She called them and broke the news. She cried over the phone and promised she would drive up to see them every weekend and that no matter what, they would always be friends and would keep in touch.

For years her mother had single handedly managed their Atlanta office. Her father never hired extra office help in the Atlanta office, so at times her mother would ask Kelly to stop by after school to help her catch up with the filing and some of the office work. Kelly would usually go straight from school to the office to see if her mother needed help. She usually ended up doing her homework there. It seemed her family spent more time at the office than they did at home. The agents who worked for them worked mainly from their homes. They usually came in a little while in the mornings or afternoons to make calls or to pick up messages. Kelly's dad had to break the news to them that he had decided to move to Birmingham and that he would leave Dan

Carter, his senior agent in charge of running things during their move. He told them he was not selling the company and that he would continue to commute back and forth as he had always done. Towards the end of August he had some movers come and move some of his furniture and files to the Birmingham office. At that time Kelly's parents had still not found a house so they decided to move in with grandmother Birdie until they could find what they were looking for.

At the time of Kelly's grandfather's death he had seven agents working for him. Kelly's dad had said it was the largest crew he had ever had. Since Grandmother Birdie had closed the office the day of her grandfather's death and said she had not had contact with any of the agents since the funeral, Kelly's father called each one and met with them and they all returned to work at the office. She could remember how everything seemed to be fine at first, but eventually one by one they all left the company. She guessed it was because of being under different management even though it was her dad who had been their Sales Manager. As it was, eventually new agents were hired. In order to become an agent you had to have your real estate license or be prepared to take the final exam. Kelly saw many potential agents come and go. Office help was always needed and she was asked to work five days a week. Summertime had come and gone and almost another year had passed before she realized it.

All she had were fleeting memories of the life she had left behind in Atlanta. Since they had moved to Birmingham she had only been able to go to Atlanta one time to visit with Regina and Linda and that was only for a couple of hours when her mother dropped her off at Regina's on her way to see a close friend who was in the hospital there. While waiting on her mother to pick her up at Regina's for some reason Kelly begin thinking about her mother being upset because someone she knew was sick with Lupus. "Lupus?" Kelly thought. "What is that?" When her mother picked her up Kelly asked how Sharon was doing and then before her mom could answer Kelly asked; "What is

Lupus?" Her mother replied, "What is Lupus?" "How did you know Sharon has Lupus?" "I guess you told me" said Kelly. "No, I don't think I did" replied her mother. "Well, I don't know" replied Kelly. "Well, said her mom, Sharon does have Lupus. I'm not really sure about all the details myself. I just know she is very sick and I just hope she gets better." "Me too" said Kelly.

Since her grandfather's passing, her parents had tried to stay focused on keeping both businesses running. She knew that for right then that was pretty much the way it had to be. Her parents had needed her total unconditional support and she had been fine with that. She always tried helping them in any way she could. They had both been so busy neither had mentioned college options and she hadn't brought up the subject but she knew it was about time she did.

Kelly was now nineteen. Surely her parents could see that she was growing in more ways than one as she became more mature and independent with the passing months. She was becoming more self motivated with high aspirations and dreams to accomplish great things during her life. But at that time in her life, above all, she was a teenager for God's sake and walked around most of the time feeling like a caged animal. She just wanted to break free and to begin living her life outside of her parents' supervision. She needed to be accepted as her own person. She longed for a greater sense of self accomplishment. Sometimes she would think that after getting her college degree, maybe moving back to Atlanta, and getting an apartment with maybe Regina or Linda. She longed to be living out on her own, but she knew that for now she had to focus on college options in Birmingham. She knew either Sanford University or the University of Alabama in Tuscaloosa would be her most likely choices so she started to make plans.

CHAPTER 5

Kelly was trying to live a normal teenager's life while coping with constant premonitions that gave her migraine headaches from dealing with the stream of endless thoughts that cluttered her mind during both day and night. She felt no one would ever understand what she was going through so she kept the premonitions that came in dreams and thoughts to herself. She had tried to make a point of never discussing her psychic abilities with her parents because she didn't feel they would ever understand. So, she tried to keep it a secret that she had recently begun doing research on people with psychic abilities, well known clairvoyants, and reading some books on the paranormal. She tried not to let those types of books influence her but she was searching for evidence to explain why she had her abilities. She knew her search would never end. Since moving to Birmingham, her dreams and the array of constant thoughts that consistently streamed through her mind during the day and disturbing her sleep at night, had increased and she had begun suffering from anxiety headaches.

At times she would have to take a few minutes in the afternoon and lie down, close her eyes and rest. She soon learned to meditate. She had a book on meditation techniques that she followed to try and slow her thoughts down to relax. She would start out by relaxing her body all over as this meditation book she had instructed. She would take deep breaths and become fully relaxed and try to slow down her thought process. After a couple of years of using meditation techniques she then found herself creating a place of retreat in her mind. Little by little her place of retreat began to come more into focus. One afternoon when she had gotten herself completely relaxed she could see herself walking through a small bright white room. In the room on the left wall was a small window. She glanced outside as she slowly walked by the window. She could see the sun was shining and could tell the weather was warm outside. In her mind it was a summer day. When she reached the door entrance at the end of the room there was no door only a doorway. Only thick black darkness lay ahead at the doorway. She stood with both feet together and glanced to the right down a long dark narrow hallway. She couldn't see light at the far end nor could she see the end. She looked to the left. Only a few steps away was a heavy wooden door with a small window at the top. She stepped into the dark hallway and looked out the window. She saw what appeared to be a garden. She opened the door and walked outside. She felt a soft warm breeze sweeping over her face. She was filled with a pleasant feeling of tranquility.

Across the way she could see a door and she had the feeling there were other people nearby as she could imagine them scurrying about. She looked around but saw no one. She was standing in what seemed to be a courtyard with a stone floor. She could tell it was about mid morning because the sun began to grow brighter and the stone floor was warming up although many of the stones felt very cool beneath her feet. The walls of the building appeared to be made with flat stones enclosed with cement or hard dirt. As she looked around she could see there was another door to her right. She listened but could hear no sounds of life coming from behind it. To her left was a narrow stone walkway and to the right of the walkway was an area that had a high wall that also appeared to be fashioned from some type of cement. The wall was cracked and weathered looking and was covered in vines, green plants and wild flowers. The high wall made it secluded and private. She turned to her left and walked down the pathway alongside the high wall to an entrance. As she walked she could feel every stone and crack beneath her feet and even the soft feel of dirt as some of it clung to the bottom of her feet.

As she entered into the secluded area she could see there were several old wooden tables and cement seats positioned around what looked like a small arena area. Far to the right next to the back wall sat a man on a huge flat rock in a long robe. Kelly could not look at his face. The only part of him that seemed to be visible to her was his bare feet. She knew this man was Jesus. This was a surprise to her because she didn't know until that moment that this event was going to occur and she had not had a prior premonition that any part of this mediation experience would occur. She went over to him and knelt down. She stayed in a kneeling position for a long while, with her eyes closed and her head bent down. The experience seemed so real that for a few minutes she felt she had stepped back in time to a place that had once existed.

As she knelt and prayed for forgiveness and guidance she could feel a slight gentle summer breeze caressing her face, gently lifting up the sides of her hair. As she was kneeing and praying for forgiveness and guidance, she wondered how her imagination had discovered this place of worship. Had this sanctuary existed somewhere hidden in her mind? Why had she come here? Why now was she pursuing this setting for meditation? Had she searched for it somewhere in her mind? Was it easy for her imagination to find or had she crossed over a barrier to find it? She began to elaborate: "Possibly, she thought, somewhere in ancient times a similar place of prayer may have once existed and it is possible that it still does. Maybe in the memories of time this stone garden with the high secluded wall may have really existed and was a place where Jesus taught the word of God."

Kelly decided this place of solitude was simply a place she had created for herself for a time of prayer and consolation. She decided the garden surroundings were created in her mind and was a good thing because it gave her a private place to meditate and pray. She felt happy and content that she had creatively discovered this sanctuary for prayer because she knew from then on she would not be without the inter strength she needed and the guidance she had been praying for. She meditated a while longer and continued quietly praying for forgiveness, inner strength and guidance and then ended her meditation.

From that day on whenever things seemed to get too much for her she would retreat to her quiet place and pray. It was her time out, her place of solitude, a place where she felt safe and no one or no other outside force could destroy it or take it from her. Soon the meditations became a part of her weekly routine.

CHAPTER 6

Whenever Kelly started on a project or made plans to accomplish something she became determined and was anxious for results. She had started thinking more and more about starting college. She longed to move forward, but felt she was stranded in the daily routine of working in her parent's business. Then one afternoon while at the office a girl around Kelly's age came in. She asked if she could fill out an employment application. It was very seldom that someone inquired about an office position at their company especially since her parents never advertised for office help. Kelly couldn't believe her ears. She thought to herself; "I want to go to college, and what I need right now is someone to fill my position here." Kelly handed her a legal pad to jot down references. Her name was Kim. They hit it off right away. She told Kelly she had worked as an apartment leasing agent in her hometown in North Alabama. She had moved to Birmingham because she had been hired through an ad in the paper as an assistant manager at an apartment complex in the Southside area but said when she got to the job location things didn't work out.

She was recently divorced and had a two year old daughter to support. She was unable to get steady child support from her ex-husband. She had taken him to court several times and even had him thrown in jail but it didn't do any good. He would make a couple of support payments and then quit his job and leave town. She was living with her grandparents in Birmingham but said that the arrangement wasn't working out either because at night her baby would sometimes wake them up with her crying. She seemed depressed and said she had been looking for work everywhere and she needed to get an apartment. She told Kelly she had always been interested in selling real estate and thought if she worked for a real estate company and got some office experience maybe later she could become a real estate agent. Kelly could see that she had already had a hard life for someone so young. She was impressed that her goal was to become a real estate agent and told her she would talk to her father and see if she could help.

Kelly knew how her dad felt about hiring office help but wanted to try and persuade him anyway. That afternoon when he came in to close up, she picked up Kim's application and walked slowly towards him studying his face to see if she could tell what kind of mood he was in. He looked tired. "Dad, she said softly, you know I've been thinking, now that we're pretty much settled in here, and I've been thinking about college again. I want to go to Sanford University and get an accounting degree." "Well, he said nodding his head up and down that sounds good, if that's where you want to go. You need to get started on that degree." "I know she replied. I'll go down there next week and talk to a counselor about enrolling. Oh, by the way, I met this girl today. She came in looking for a job. She's from Fort Payne." Kelly laid the legal pad on the desk in front of him and continued. "She said she had a job working as an apartment leasing agent in Fort Payne. She's divorced and is trying to raise her little two year old daughter by herself.

She said she'd work full time or part time. You know we'll need some office help since I am going to start school. Of course I will still help mother out here as much as I can." Kelly was amazed that she actually blurted that entire sentence out in one breath to her father. He just listened while looking down at the pad at Kim's information. Kelly was glad that she had been a little forceful and hoped that he would come around to thinking it was a good idea. She then added before she hurried out of the office, "We'll need to hire some extra help if I'm going to start school." So Kelly felt she could go ahead with her plans. The following week she visited Sanford and filled out enrollment forms for the next quarter.

CHAPTER 7

Kelly's mother had not been feeling well for weeks. After repeated visits to her doctor she was finally diagnosed with Lupus. Kelly couldn't believe that her mother had the same illness as her friend Sharon and Kelly remembered she had thought her mother was worried about someone who had Lupus when she was visiting her friend in the hospital. She wondered if her mother suspected or even knew that she herself might have it then. Kelly could tell her mother was very upset when she gave the news to Kelly. Her eyes welled up with tears. Kelly could tell that she was really worried because her friend had actually died from complications of the disease in the hospital. Kelly asked, "How serious is it?" Her mother replied, "Well, it can be controlled with medications. I will be fine. It will just take time." There were days that followed that her mother didn't feel like coming to the office.

The next week Kelly mentioned to her about Kim coming in looking for a job. She told her mother she had given Kim's references to her father and told her she had also talked to him about her starting to Sanford the next quarter and that he had given his approval. Kelly told her mother she hoped she would agree with him. Her mother said she did agree and that Kelly needed to go ahead and enroll and that she also needed to call Kim to see if she still needed a job. She said she would speak with Albert about hiring Kim. She said since she had been out sick the past week and didn't know how long it would be before she would feel well enough to work her usual hours, they would need to hire extra help. A few weeks passed and they finally hired Kim full time.

In time Kelly was able to obtain her accounting degree and while still in college began working for a CPA firm. She worked there for nine years. She bought a townhouse in the Southside area of Birmingham that was not far from her parents. It was during that time her grandmother Birdie had a couple of strokes. The first one paralyzed the right side of her face and affected her speech and the second one paralyzed the right side of her body. She had to move in with Kelly's parents and she stayed in Kelly's old room. A year or so later she had a third stroke and while in the hospital developed pneumonia and died. Kelly's dad put his parent's house up for sale. Kelly thought it was sad since it was the house he grew up in and where all of his childhood memories were as well as all the memories that she had of spending part of her summer vacations there with her grandparents almost every summer when she was a little girl. He hated to sell it, but since he was an only child with no relatives who were interested in buying, he had to put it on the market.

CHAPTER 8

The psychic premonitions that Kelly had experienced as a young girl had remained constant as she grew older. She realized she would never get use to the mental upheaval that had become her way of life. She tried to adjust but had to continue with the practice of her meditation techniques in order to get some relief from the reoccurring migraines that would usually occur after a dream. Through the meditations she kept her life somewhat in order and considered her life fairly normal although it would be absurd to think that anyone standing out and looking in at her life would agree that someone who had daily psychic experiences could have a normal existence.

On one occasion while driving home from work, Kelly suddenly saw in her mind a little dog running across a road. She then pictured a lady running behind the dog. Kelly was driving her usual route home. As she topped the hill on the street where she lived, she came to a quick halt at the stop sign and then took a sharp right dipping down the steep hill that lead to the end of the cul-de-sac street where she lived. Suddenly from out of know where appeared a small dog that dashed out in front of her car. She slammed on the brakes hard enough that the seat bumped her back and her head upward hitting the car headboard and lunging her forward onto the steering wheel. At the same time a lady ran out in front of her car chasing after the dog. Kelly felt that if she had not had that sudden premonition only seconds before she might have hit the dog as well as the owner.

Some weeks later while driving up the same hill near her home, she saw a lady walking down the sidewalk on the hill. At a glance Kelly was taken back for a moment because she looked exactly like her Aunt Carol, her mother's sister. This lady had her aunt's same wavy strawberry blonde hair and her physical features resembled her to a tee. She was smiling at someone as she crossed the street. Kelly drove slowly watching her take a long draw from her cigarette. She smiled and displayed a so familiar larger than life smile that went from ear to ear just like her aunt's. Kelly thought wow, the resemblance is really uncanny. She knew of course it wasn't her aunt since she lived in Atlanta. She couldn't wait to call her mother when she got home to tell her about seeing her Aunt Carol's twin. When she arrived home her phone was ringing. It was her mother.

She said Aunt Carol had been taken to the hospital with chest pains and had been admitted to have emergency by-pass surgery. Before she had thought, Kelly told her about the lady she saw on her way home and how she had resembled her aunt. Her mother began crying and Kelly apologized to her and said she was sorry and didn't mean to upset her more than she was already upset. "That was really bad timing on my part" Kelly thought. Although the news her mother had just received about Aunt Carol had been very upsetting to her mother, it never occurred to her mother that Kelly might have had a premonition about her aunt or that her aunt was somehow trying to reach out to them in her thoughts. Kelly just happened to be the receiver of her aunt's thoughts.

CHAPTER 9

Kelly was remembering back as she parked her car in front of the real estate office that morning that it had now been eleven years since they had moved to Birmingham. She couldn't believe all that time had gone by since they had moved from Atlanta. She entered the office and there sat Kim studying for her real estate exam. Kelly remembered that on the day she meet her, Kim had said she hoped one day to become an agent. Kelly could see Kim's excitement knowing that she was at last studying and the end results were in sight. Kim asked Kelly if she would consider taking the exam as well and they could be study partners. Kelly had of course pondered the idea many times before. Now that she had finished college and felt secure enough in her accounting career, why not get licensed in the business? "That's sound great said Kelly. We can be study partners."

Her dad was very pleased with her decision to get her license. She couldn't wait to tell him when she passed the exam. He grinned and gave her a big hug. "That's my little girl" he said squeezing and shaking her by the shoulders. It was like he thought she had finally come to her senses. He said "Kelly you already know this business but now you can have it all. You know, we always planned, you know, for the business to be yours after me and your mother retire. That is if you want it." Kelly smiled and said "I know dad, we'll talk sometime." Although her father had never mentioned her taking over the business before, Kelly knew her parents planned that she would inherit their business one day. She had also had the realization that it was one of the reasons Kelly's dad did not want his mother to sell his dad's business. He wanted to keep it in the family if possible. But, at that time in her life she didn't want to give any serious thought to running their business. She just wanted to live her own life in her own way and enjoy it as much as possible.

Her mother was a member of the City Beautification Board and the Historic Preservation Society. After Kelly had gotten her real estate license her mother began encouraging her to attend some of the meetings with her. She finally decided to please her mother and attended one of the Historic Society meetings with her. To her surprise she really enjoyed the meeting. She found that many of the members were very interesting people and she enjoyed the topics of discussion and soon began looking forward to attending the meetings with her mother.

She soon became very interested in architectural design. She became fascinated with things like building structures, interior room layouts and was really drawn to homes built in the 1700 and 1800's with grand column structures. She was fascinated with the many different styles of old homes and the eras they were constructed in from all over the world. Her favorites though had to be the Colonial style homes like the Georgian, the Federal, the Colonial and Greek revival styles. Of course the scary Queen Ann was the most intriguing but she knew she would never live in one of those because the gingerbread design had the spooky thing going on. Something she noticed was that in the South you can take a house design from anywhere in the world and turn it into a perfect southern home with just a few pieces of southern décor. She was a southern girl brought up with southern traditions so one of the things that most excited her was the old southern heritage type homes. The older the house the more it intrigued her. She loved to explore old homes venturing which décor would have been suitable for that home during that particular period in history. She read about traditional southern living in history books, on the internet, and on several occasions had the opportunity to look through a few old antebellum homes that were on the market. If an old southern home was still in tack or had been restored back to its original splendor, she was in awe. It was an adventure to explore the interior wall design, to the view the original wood floors, the old kitchens, and to admire the beautiful wooden mantels.

History was also important. She wanted to know who designed the house, the year it was built, where it was located and especially who the residents were and how long they lived there and if there were any interesting stories behind the home. She wanted to see pictures of houses and pictures of the inhabitants. She also did research at the library, book stores and on the internet for old homes from the Civil War days. She was intrigued with Civil War stories. She would examine pictures of beautiful old antebellum homes that had survived the ravages of the Civil War or served as headquarters for soldiers. She started a collection of books on architecture, interior design and even books on ghost stories that might be included if part of the in-depth history of an old southern home.

CHAPTER 10

She continued to attend some of the different meetings with her mother but after a few months had passed, her mother's condition began to escalate and she took a turn for the worse. She had spent a week in the hospital and upon returning home seemed tired all the time while her medications made her depressed and even agitated. Kelly had also noticed a change in her dad. He found out his blood pressure was too high and his doctor told him to change his diet and start relaxing more. He decided to sell the Atlanta office to Dan. Her mother had been working only 3 days a week and now her father had decided to cut back his work week as well. Fortunately they could rely on Kim and Kelly to handle the office and some agent responsibilities. Her parents bought a camper and a camcorder. They had decided to relax and recoup during that summer and talked about future plans to travel to Montana in the camper to sightsee for a couple of months.

They had set their sites for November. Her dad said it was time they started taking some vacation time for themselves. They had decided to go to New Orleans for the regional real estate convention for a last hoorah to celebrate their semi-retiring and to get out their "feelers" for their new camper although he said they would rent a hotel room while they were there. Kelly's mother told her they planned to drive down that coming Tuesday morning for the convention on Wednesday morning, visit the French Quarters Wednesday afternoon, spend the night there and start back around noon on Thursday. Kelly said she would take off to help Kim out in the office while they were away. They left for New Orleans early that Tuesday morning and called Kelly after they arrived. Her mother called her again Wednesday evening to see how things had gone back at the office that day and said they were having a really good time. She said they had just returned from the French Quarters and were getting ready for bed. She said she would call Kelly at the office Thursday before they headed back to Birmingham.

Around 3:00 am on Thursday morning, Kelly woke up with an extremely bad migraine. "Oh" she moaned and thought this was one of the worst ones she had ever had. She had been dreaming about her parents. She remembered she was in a large fenced in area like a parking lot where old cars and trucks were parked. It was like a junkyard. It was night time in her dream. She could see herself in the dream walking through tall grass, when she spotted an old camper with the right side door wide open. She walked up to it and peered in. It was very dark inside. A man who she did not recognize came up behind her and asked who she was looking for. She explained her mother and father use to have a camper that looked very much like that one. She told him that she thought it might be theirs.

Parts of her dream were fuzzy and she could only remember pieces of it that stood out. The next thing she remembered was she saw herself driving down the road in that old camper. She stopped because she was suddenly blinded by bright lights and couldn't see where she was going. She could hear voices talking outside the camper. She lay in bed with her eyes closed and her head pounding. She tried to remember more of the dream but the pain on the left side of her head was too great. Her temples were now pulsating so she turned the bedside light on, got up and took some migraine medicine and eventually drifted back to sleep.

When her alarm went off at 5:00 AM, she awoke not feeling much better and kept reliving portions of the same dream as she got ready and rushed off to the office. She and Kim had a fairly busy day and it had flown by fast. All day long she had butterflies in her stomach as the migraine lingered on. Before she realized, it was already 3:00 PM. She wondered why her mother had not called her like she said she would before they started back to Birmingham. She called her mother's cell and left a message for her to call her but she never called her back. Kelly became very concerned. By 5:00 PM she was sitting impatiently in bumper to bumper traffic headed for home. She called her mother's cell phone again but it switched to her voice mail. She said "Hi mom it's Kelly." "I'm worried about you and dad." "You never called me." "When you get this, call me and let me know where you are ok?" "Please call me on my cell - I love you."

It was October and darkness had already engulfed the now lighted string of cars that stretched out for miles down the road as far as she could see disappearing over the hills that lay for miles beyond and in the back of her as she witnessed through her rear view mirror. She felt cold so she switched the car heater on for a minute to take off the chill. Her thoughts drifted to her parents once again. She was glad they had decided to get away for some long needed time together. Her mind went back to the afternoon when she told her dad she had passed the insurance exam. She pictured him grinning and hugging her. It was worth going through the course just to see how proud he seemed to be. At that moment her eyes welled up with tears as she thought of her mother. Even though she had been sick, she had still continued to try and stay close and connected to Kelly making sure they always had plans to enjoy a few activities together. She longed to tell her how much she loved and appreciated her. She decided she would bake a coconut cake, her mother's favorite and take it over that coming weekend. She kept pushing away the feeling of doom that was welling up in her stomach.

As soon as she pulled in her driveway she called her mom again but still no answer. She didn't know her dad's new cell phone number and wondered why she hadn't asked him for it. When she got in the house she called the hotel in New Orleans. They said her parents had checked out at 11:00 AM that morning. Kelly was positive then that something bad had to have happened because her mother would have called her by now. She had known all day in the back of her mind that something just wasn't right. She had been thinking about that horrible dream all day long. She had gotten the worst migraine that she had ever had and her mother had never called her. She just kept praying that they were alright. She called the hotel back and told them what she suspected and asked them for the police department's number.

She then called the New Orleans police station and gave them her parent's names and description of their camper and inquired about any accidents occurring on Wednesday night or Thursday. They said they would be back in touch with her once they ran a check. Around 8:00 PM that evening the phone rang. It was the New Orleans police department. The officer said there were three motorists involved in a collision that day but that they could not make a definite identification over the phone. He said that they believed one party had now been identified at the hospital morgue but the other two had not. He said Kelly would need to come down in person to identify these individuals as her family members. They said they could not give her the description of the vehicles involved. Kelly talked to an officer in charge and told him her situation and that she was in Birmingham and wanted to make sure these two people were her parents before she drove down there. The officer had her mother's purse and read her driver's license information to Kelly.

Kelly felt sick as she sat down on the edge of the bed. The hurt she felt in her heart was unbearable. She just sat there in a daze as he repeated the name and address on her mother's license. Kelly knew she had just been given the dreadful news that her parents had been killed coming back to Birmingham. She was asked to come down to the hospital morgue to identify their bodies. She was in shock and knew she shouldn't be driving down there alone so she asked Kim to go with her. The entire trip to New Orleans and to the hospital seemed like a dream to Kelly. When they arrived she saw the bodies and confirmed they were her parents. She stood dazed as she read the police report over and over again. It said a witness told the police they had heard the diesel truck's tire blow out as the driver crossed the median flying at fast speed hitting the camper head on. It was thought at that time that both people in the camper were killed instantly. The driver of the truck was thrown from the truck and also died at the scene of the accident. The dream Kelly had about the camper kept resurfacing in her mind.

CHAPTER II

Kelly realized the day after their funeral as she stood alone in the large warehouse that was part of the old Brown Real Estate building how her parents had prepared her all those years for that moment, the moment she would be taking control of the business. Although she would have never imagined that it would come with their lives ending in such a horrible, unspeakable way. During the past few days she had spent with her Grandmother Evelyn and her mother's sister Aunt Carol preparing for the funeral. She had grieved quietly at the funeral home as relatives and friends squeezed and patted her hands, hugged her and gave their condolences. Now In the dead quiet of the dusty old office building she sat alone. She prayed over and over for her parents. She prayed aloud to God. "God please forgive them for their sins. You know they were both wonderful, good people." With tears welled in her eyes she walked up and down looking around in the dimly lit office wondering what she should do next.

She had made an appointment with their attorney to read their wills the following week. She wasn't prepared for the responsibilities that lay ahead but she knew she had to keep the business going. On the front counter lay a stack of mail. She thought of her mother and tears streamed down her face. She suddenly hurt all over. She remembered how when she was in grammar school she would take the mail to her mother to be opened. She remembered how she had looked up to her, depended on her and realized that her mother had actually been her greatest role model and had instilled her with a lot of self confidence. "Or was it my dad?" she thought.

"My dad, he was the one always so full of energy, drive and determination. He was never satisfied until he reached his goal. He continuously pushed and pushed for more and more." That was her father, always too busy to be bothered but had always been so generous to her just like her grandfather had been. She realized she had loved him for the person he was and for the person he wanted her to become. Kelly hoped she had truly inherited some of his inner strength with what she felt must lay ahead of her. She thought, "I must keep the business going by taking things one day at a time because I can hear him telling me that is what I should do." "Monday, I'll unlock the door as usual, turn the open sign over and life will go on." "Oh sure it will" she cried. "I don't really see how, but it will."

She remembered when her grandfather passed and how her dad took over his business. She knew now how he must have felt having such a great burden put on his shoulders. The feeling of dread and fear that must have come over him that had now come over her. She sat down and thought, "But he didn't think twice." "He took over granddaddy's business and gave up his own." Kelly suddenly had a realization that her parent's business would now possibly be her main livelihood. She proclaimed to herself that she had inherited the inner strength of her father and mother and that they were with her and would always be with her. And the Lord was with her so she would be alright. She stood up and wiped the tears from her cheeks but she couldn't contain her mental anguish and she began to cry again.

The Passage Part II

CHAPTER 12

The alarm clock screamed loudly. With her eyes closed Kelly reached over in the dark and turned it off. She lay back on her pillow and began rethinking the dream she just had. She awoke with a headache and felt sick to her stomach, the way some premonition dreams left her feeling. She dreamed she was in a big house. She could remember standing in the middle of a large empty room and looking up at glistening lights that reflected from a sparkling chandelier that hung high from a dark ceiling. The long pieces of clear prism glass tinkled quietly one then another as the chandelier gently swayed to a light breeze. The room was dark and appeared fairly large with the far end the darkest disappearing down a long hallway that had doors on both sides of it. She could hear voices and footsteps approaching in the distance. A voice told her a man was searching for her and that he had to tell her something important and wanted to give her a key. She tried searching for the man down the dark hallway but she struggled as she walked. She felt like her legs were being held and she couldn't go down the hall.

In the dream she stretched her arms out before her one at a time as though she was swimming through deep water. She stood in the hallway and tried to open door after door but they were all locked. She was looking for this man and she felt like he was in the house but he was hiding from someone, not her but from someone else. There was a glimmer of light at the end of the long hallway and in one part of her dream she thought she caught a glimpse of a man at the far end as a door suddenly opened to reveal what looked like a garden. She could see two distant figures standing, engaged in a conversation. One of the men stopped talking for a moment and glanced her way. When she tried to walk down the hall again they both disappeared. She lay in bed trying to ponder the meaning of the dream. Her arms and legs felt very tired.

Suddenly her eyes flew wide open when her two little dogs began jumping up and down playfully trying to get on her bed. She pulled each one of them up and gave them a hug. Since her parents had passed she had become quiet lonely and had gotten two Pekinese puppies for companionship. "Oh God she moaned. I've got so much to do today girls. Come on, we'd better get going." It was Saturday and she had promised to attend a meeting with the Historic Preservation Committee. After her mother's death she had promised the members she would continue to attend the meetings and help with some of the events. Although, she was not interested in taking on a demanding position like her mother had on the committee, at the same time she had gotten use to going to the meetings with her mother and she felt somehow she was carrying on a tradition for her by continuing to participate in some of the meetings and activities.

She also enjoyed helping and playing a part in the restoration of some of the beautiful old homes and buildings in Birmingham. She hated to see any of them torn down especially if they were of historical importance. She worked with a good team of ladies whose goal was saving some of the old southern historical homes, and buildings including some organizations and churches in parts of the city as part of the city preservation work. Kelly was drawn to the big two story houses that had window seats and fireplaces in the dining rooms and bedrooms. She loved the cold creaking wooden floors, high ceilings with chandeliers, tall windows and long porches. She found them more than historically beautiful. She felt they were like living entities that demanded constant respect and felt it was an obligation for one to feel humble in their presence. As long as even one of these old places stood even partially intact their enchantment would remain strong and everlasting as would the time in history that surrounded each one including the families that had once inhabited them.

Her interest or obsession had grown so that she had decided she was tired of townhouse living and she wanted to start looking around for and old restored home of her own. Kelly of course had in mind her own old historic type of home, and preferred a real classic vintage style. She wanted one that was the epitome of the traditional southern mansion home and she was willing to wait for the right one to go on the market. In the past she had several opportunities to buy a number of old houses but had never been interested in doing that before. At the meeting she saw some new faces and a familiar one, Louise Westbrook whom she had seen a couple of times when she had been to past meetings with her mother. Kelly noticed Ms. Westbrook had pinned up a picture of a beautiful old house on the bulletin board. Kelly got out of her seat to study the picture for a moment. "This is really a beautiful house, she thought. I believe it would be considered a Colonial Georgian style." She smiled. From the picture you could tell the house had one of those large extended porches with four huge round columns on the front porch. "Wow" she said softly, then giggled to herself. "It looks almost like Tara." She eyed the price. Even though she had not seen the house, she still explored the idea of charming Mrs. Westbrook down on the price. Yes, she was her daddy's girl.

She wrote down the address and returned to her seat. At the luncheon she sat down beside Mrs. Westbrook and after introducing herself remarked how beautiful the house looked from the pictures. She smiled at Mrs. Westbrook and said, "It looks like Tara". "Your right" replied Mrs. Westbrook. She wanted to bring to Mrs. Westbrook's attention that she was the daughter of Albert Brown, of Brown Real Estate, and that her mother had been treasure of the committee but before Kelly could mention it, Mrs. Westbrook said that she had known her mother and remembered seeing Kelly with her at few of the meetings. Mrs. Westbrook said she had heard about the horrible accident and said how sorry she was for her loss.

Kelly thanked her for her condolences and laid one of the pictures of the house Mrs. Westbrook had brought on her lap. Mrs. Westbrook glanced at the picture and began to tell Kelly how she and husband had originally bought the house from the previous owner five years ago to present as a wedding gift to their daughter Faye and her fiancé. "They were to have been married that following summer said Mrs. Westbrook but the wedding never took place because my daughter's run-around, no good for nothing fiancé couldn't be faithful during their engagement. So, when she found out what was going on behind her back, she called the wedding off. It was really a shame because Faye idolized that boy, and we had grown fond of him too. They had been engaged for two years" Mrs. Westbrook continued.

"Her father put a lot of time and effort into restoring that house. You should see the inside. It is absolutely breathtaking. You drive up and you're looking at a great big beautiful mansion sitting right in the center of the block in Southside, surrounded by other old homes but that could never compare. We tried renting if for awhile but that didn't work out. There are just too many rough people out there that tear up things. It would make a wonderful bed and breakfast, she added but you can't get it zoned in that area. Anyway, it has been vacant now for over a year. Marvin was working over there this past week replacing faucets and bathroom fixtures. It's going on the market in just a couple of days. We're finally ready to sell." "Well from the picture, said Kelly, it could be exactly what I might be interested in for myself."

"Well, as you know, said Mrs. Westbrook there are many beautiful old homes in the Southside area but you won't find another house like this one. It has been completely restored. It has received the beautification award. You can see from the picture there is a large front yard and the back yard is quite big as well." In all she said there's about one acre of land. She held up the picture to Kelly "You can see in the picture the back yard is fenced in. You can park in the back of the house off the street and it's also in a safe quiet neighborhood." "It sounds perfect" replied Kelly. "Would you mind if I drive over and look at it?" "Are you looking for yourself?" asked Mrs. Westbrook. "Yes mam, I might be interested in it for myself," Kelly replied. "Why of course dear, Mrs. Westbrook replied. I believe Marvin has been putting a front door key under the porch mat." "Well, Kelly replied, I could drive by there today on my way home." "Ok, I will call Marvin and tell him you'll be coming by. He may drop by to talk with you while you're looking." "Ok, that will be fine, said Kelly. I think when the meeting is over I will go on and head that way."

CHAPTER 13

The house was located in an older neighborhood in Southside of Birmingham on a crowded street with similar types of old two story houses with colors ranging from white, yellow, blue and green. Kelly was hoping she would have a chance to look at the house before Mr. Westbrook arrived. She drove slowly viewing the homes on both sides of the street. The street was narrow with cars parked on both sides and hardly no way two cars could drive down it at the same time. It does appear like a pleasant neighborhood thought Kelly and the front lawns look really well kept. The neighborhood also appeared very quiet. It was passed noon and not a soul was to be seen.

As she drove slowly down the street she spotted a large white antebellum house on the right located like Mrs. Westbrook had said, right in the middle of the block. Kelly couldn't see the address although she recognized it from the pictures and knew this had to be the one. She turned her car around and started back down the street again to get a closer look. She pulled over to the opposite side of the street up to the curb in front of the house still searching for the address on the front of the house, and then she saw it on the porch mail box. Kelly was in awe. It looked just like the picture except so much more beautiful. She stood in the front yard and starred up at the big white house with its huge strong towering columns. She tilted her head back to take in the beautiful blue sky that she very seldom looked at. Somehow the beautiful blue sky fit the occasion so perfectly. She suddenly felt so happy. The house was right out of a romantic novel. The huge front yard was full of healthy green grass that glistened in the sunlight like a mossy green blanket. A large magnolia tree hovered towards the house from the edge of the side walk.

She shaded her eyes with her hand as the sun beamed down on her face and as she gazed up at the dark grey roof that slanted downward framing the three doubled upstairs windows. The huge front door revealed a beautiful fan shaped crystal glass window above it and on each side of the door were long narrow windows that were covered with white lacy curtains. All of the front windows had black shutters. Middle way on the roof top there were two tall chimneys paralleled to each other. She assumed these were the authentic chimneys. There must be an attic she thought because the roof is so high. The house had a long gray wooden porch that extended the full length of the huge mansion and as she gazed upward again she could see the four colossal white columns that were supporting the roof.

She quickly climbed the stairs to the porch. She tried to peer into one of the narrow windows beside the door but couldn't see anything through the curtains. She turned her head and viewed each side of the long porch then turned around and looked out into street. She walked the full length of the creaking porch, leaning over the sides to see what she could see of the back yard as well as the neighbor's yards. She returned to the front door. The large front door was dark mahogany. She stood on her toes and ran her fingers across the fan shaped window of crystal patterned glass at the top of the door. Afterwards she walked to the edge of the porch beside the steps and opened her hand and placed it directly on to one of the front columns. The sight of it and the warm feel of its large smooth surface made her smile. The experience gave her a sudden feeling of accomplishment, like she had climbed to the top of a mountain and had claimed her throne. Touching it made her feel so confident.

Suddenly her senses became ignited with new energy, with a new purpose. But when she let go of the column she felt like she was falling, reaching into infinity. Touching the column had been like touching a hundred year old artifact that had been placed in a museum and had laid there forgotten and undisturbed until that very moment. It stood quiet, strong with a story untold until she touched it and invaded its private world. It didn't take but a touch and it had come alive wanting to share with her its deepest secrets. But Kelly didn't really want to know all it had to tell right then. Instead she took a deep breath and leaned against the column resting her head there as to comfort a friend and stared for awhile out into the deserted street. There was still no traffic, no sign of life. It was so quiet you could hear a pin drop.

Finally, she took another deep breath and gathered her thoughts. She would first look at the back yard before going into the house. Kelly's mother had loved a beautiful flower garden and at the beginning of each summer she would plant all types of annuals and roses and never seemed to grow tired of tending to them all in the summer, every summer. Kelly couldn't remember one year that their front and back yard wasn't covered in beautiful flowers that her mother would labor so hard to grow. Her father prided himself as well with the beautiful lawn he kept each year. She had to see the back yard of this house and imagine how beautiful her flower garden and lawn could be. Azalea bushes surrounded the front porch area. She walked around to the right side of the house where five large hibiscus bushes grew.

She hoped that in the summer when they bloomed they would be blue like the ones her grandmother Birdie had around her house so they would remind her of her grandmother and her father. But it really didn't matter that much about the color because she would love them no matter what color they were. There wasn't a gate entrance on the right side of the house but there was a small gate on the left side of the house so she walked around to the left side of the house and flipped up the gate lock and walked into the back yard. Like Mrs. Westbrook had said, the yard was enclosed with a fence, but it was a chain link fence. Kelly imagined that in the 1800's when the house was built and there was less crime in the city, when metal chain yard fences were not that necessary for family safety, there must have been a white wooden fence that framed the house making it even more beautiful. It would have adorned the house and property as was intended by the architect.

But now those days were gone and she rationalized that the paved driveway that started about ten yards from the front side gate entrance and extended to the end of the back yard to the alley gate were the newest modern additions. The back alley gate did appear to be a good idea as you could drive up to the back of the house locking the gate behind you and securing both your car and your privacy, although the alley gate had only a flip latch that secured your car and the back of the house. "Parking in the back would be a good idea," thought Kelly. "That way I can keep the car off the street, safe from being hit and it would be secured by the gate. Although my top priority would be to replace the flip locks with more secure ones." For the most part the back yard was covered with beautiful grass and eight huge crepe myrtle trees that had been growing for years. Two large climbing rose bushes clung to the two tall white wooden lattices which were positioned against the back of the house on each side of the basement door.

She imagined how beautiful the roses would look in the summer. Above one of the rose lattices on left back side of the house were four windows that were lined close together. She imagined that the room had either been a sun room full of plants or a back porch. Below the windows was the basement door and to the right of that door were the steps leading up to the back door and to the right of the steps was the patio located next to the carport. She was now very anxious about seeing the inside of the house. She returned to the front gate and walked around to the porch and retrieved the door key under the mat.

The moment the key was in her hand she began to recall the dream she had the night before. She felt her stomach turn over as suddenly parts of the dream began to flood her mind. She had not wanted to remember this dream because it left her with a sad feeling. She had dreamed she was in a house searching for someone who was trying to give her a key and now, funny, she had this key in her hand. She also remembered that this person had something important to tell her. Kelly wondered as she held the key in her hand, am I there? Is this the place I dreamed of? This is not a dream she proclaimed. This is real and I don't know if I want to be here. Should I open the door or should I put the key back under the mat and leave and never come back? By nature Kelly was curious so before she could change her mind, she put the key in and turned it.

She had butterflies in her stomach as she opened the front door and stepped in. She immediately got a feeling of déjà vu. She left the door ajar, only partly closing it and kept her hand on the door knob. She listened. She felt like she had been there before, like she was returning home. The rooms looked so familiar. More and more thoughts that she had experienced in the dream began to resurface in her mind. Her eyes caught the sparkle from a large chandelier hanging over the entrance way next to the staircase. She suddenly felt dizzy and had to take a deep breath. She needed to get some air. It seemed that the very essence of the feelings she had gotten from the dream had returned and filled her senses with a feeling of sorrow and despair.

The front door creaked as she suddenly let go of the door knob letting the heavy door shut behind her. To the right was the stairway and to the left was the living room. She stood still and listened. Her eyes followed the stairs all the way to the top. She looked at the top of the stairs to see only the dim light that must have been coming from an upstairs window. She heard the upstairs floor creaking. It sounded like someone was walking in one of the rooms. After a moment the creaking stopped. She gazed around in the living room at the high ceilings and at the detailed crown molding. On the left side of the wall was a beautifully carved oak mantel that extended up the wall above the marble fire place. What really caught Kelly's attention was a huge mirror in a golden frame that hung on a long swag rope above the old wooden mantel. The mirror hung horizontal and looked at least four feet in length. It was framed with a decorative gold leaf trim around the edges and looked like an antique.

Kelly walked to the mirror and looked at herself. The house seemed suddenly very quiet and she had an uneasy feeling like someone was watching her. She turned around slowly trying to study more details of the living room. The windows were tall and narrow and appeared to take up half of the wall space between the floor and the ceiling. The hardwood flooring looked old maybe even original. The wooden floors appeared clean and waxed but creaked with each step. Kelly walked quietly from the living room, through the dining room and into the kitchen.

The kitchen was as large as the living room. As you entered the kitchen on the left was a large old fashioned hearth where she imagined meals were prepared when the house was first built in the early eighteen hundreds and the house had no electricity. That meant the hearth had been used for years and was also the main source of heat for the kitchen until it was sealed up and the house renovated and the central heat was added. The old hearth was still beautiful and still intact but the fireplace had been covered with an old oil painting of a lake surrounded by trees with a small boy walking down a trail. The hearth was made up of shiny white ceramic tiles decorated with small yellow flowers. A heavy wooden mantel with plate grooves was hanging high above the hearth with twelve tiny white decorative plates that were lined up side by side.

The right side of the kitchen wall was lined with built in cabinets that were painted white. Kelly noticed there was a set of white china in the cabinet. Across from wall cabinet was the double sink and kitchen cabinets. The kitchen cabinets started from the left close to the back door and extended around over the kitchen sink to about the middle of the room. The cabinets had been painted white and the sink area had been made more modern looking with grey granite counter tops. There was a window above the sink that looked out over the left side of the yard above the carport. In the center of the kitchen was a large oak table with lion claw feet and four matching chairs that Kelly could tell were also antiques.

There was a large old fashioned wrought iron pot rack that hung above the table. She wondered about the furniture and why it was left in the house. From the kitchen door window she glanced out into the back yard. She had noticed about midway into the kitchen to the right was a door and had thought it was probably the basement. She opened the door into total darkness and could tell from the cool air and the musty smell that it was the basement. She didn't see a light switch on the kitchen wall for the basement so she quickly shut the door and locked it back with the single cross latch.

To the right next to the back door was another room. The door was closed. She turned the doorknob and pushed hard until it popped open. This was the room with the four windows she had wondered about while looking around in the back yard. It was a bright sunny room after all. It would be perfect she thought for her house plants and as an office. Located to the right of the entrance to that room was a small bathroom. She closed the door behind her and walked back into the kitchen. She looked around the kitchen and began opening some of the cabinets and drawers. She suddenly stopped because she began to hear trembling and rattling sounds. As she glanced around it seemed everything in the kitchen was trembling. She could see the glass panes in the china cabinet trembling and the dishes slightly shaking and knocking against the cabinet glass. The back door shook and the kitchen cabinets continued making trembling and rattling sounds. Then suddenly the sounds stopped and it got very quiet. For a moment she felt mesmerized. She stood frozen, afraid to move. She waited a few minutes before she could move while her eyes searched the room for answers. All seemed to be quiet now. She turned and walked to the back door window and looked out. "There must have been a slight earthquake" she concluded as she parted the back door curtains and starred out towards the alley way.

Just as she was about to turn and walk away, she saw a man standing in the yard beside one of the myrtle trees. He was looking up at the roof. Kelly thought, "I was just looking at that tree and I know he wasn't there before. Where did he suddenly come from?" "He has work boots on and he looks like he's surveying or something and why is he staring up at the top of the house?" she wondered. The way he was dressed made her wonder if he was sent there by Mr. Westbrook to do some repairs or maybe he was someone also interested in the house. She suddenly felt an icy cold breeze pass by her. It was like a vent was blowing cold air on her but it was winter and the air conditioner couldn't be on. She felt chilled all over. At the same time she heard someone lightly knock at the front door. She turned her head to listen for a moment and then turned back to look at the man again in the back yard but he was gone.

"He couldn't have disappeared that fast" she thought. "Where did he go?" "That must be Mr. Westbrook at the door" she thought so she rushed to the living room and peered out the small window beside the front door but no one was on the porch. "I guess I'm hearing things" she said to herself, shrugging her shoulders although she could have sworn she heard a clear knock at the door. She glanced out the front door window one last time, and then rushed up the stairs to take a look at the bedrooms before Mr. Westbrook arrived. "Maybe he isn't even coming" she thought. At the top of the stairs she opened the door on the right. It was the master bedroom and more furniture. She was taken back by a large four poster canopy bed with swirling columns that almost touched the ceiling. She walked around the room and then peered into the tiny bedroom closet.

Across from that bedroom was another bedroom not quite as large. That room had a fireplace. She walked down the hall and glanced in at a third bedroom that was smaller than the other two but had a good view of the back yard. Kelly knew she probably didn't need three bedrooms but if you buy an old house that's what you're going to get, large rooms with very little closet space. At the end of the hall to the left was a bathroom with a large deep bathtub with claw feet. The tub and the old oval sink had shiny ornate brass faucets that looked like new additions. A shower had been added to the third smaller upstairs bedroom and all the fixtures appeared new as well. As Kelly walked back down the hall to the stairs she saw a knotted rope hanging from the ceiling. "Oh, the attic, she said aloud. I could store all my Christmas decorations up there."

This time she knew she heard someone on the front porch. "That must be Mr. Westbrook" she thought and rushed down the stairs to greet him at the door. "Hello" she said smiling from ear to ear. "Are you Mr. Westbrook?" The old man slowly moved his head up and down. "Well, she said it's nice to meet you. My name is Kelly Brown. I guess Mrs. Westbrook told you that I talked with her at the Historical Committee meeting this morning. I saw the pictures of this house and I had to come see it. It is really beautiful. I can tell you have been working really hard on it." Kelly was nervous so she rambled on. As he listened to Kelly the old man's somber face never changed expressions. When she came up for air he lifted his head and glanced up at her face. He looked into her eyes, his glasses resting low on his nose. "Well, it's an old house" he said as he walked to the center of the living room. He glanced at the staircase his eyes shifting left to right. He continued, "We tried renting it. We was gona make two apartments out of it but never did. Do you have a family?" he asked. His mouth dropped open as he looked at Kelly. "No sir, Kelly replied, not yet, that is, I'm not married. It would just be me and my two dogs for right now." "Are you interested in buying the house he asked?" "Well, I might be" Kelly said. Mr. Westbrook rolled his eyes and replied, "Well, I put in a new heating and air conditioning system two year ago. The roof is about six year old."

"Yes, I noticed the roof looks new" said Kelly. "Yeah, almost new he grunted. These wood floors are still in pretty good shape too" he added and some of flooring had to be replaced over the years. After all, this house is over a hundred year old. I think in all it looks pretty darn good for a hundred year old house. I guess you have looked around, but come on, I'll give you a quick tour." He began walking slowly towards the kitchen and glanced over at the fireplace. "Is the fireplace in working order?" asked Kelly.

"The fireplace works with gas logs now" he replied. "We sealed up the real fire places and the chimneys some years ago. This one here and the one upstairs both use gas logs. They have both been closed off. You can use the gas logs in there or you can use the central heat." "You might want to get a security system installed if you'd be here by yourself. He continued; it's still a pretty safe area around here but if you're gonna be living by yourself..." "Yes sir, that's a good idea" Kelly replied. "I would definitely need a security system installed."

He entered the kitchen with Kelly not far behind him. He walked over to the sink and looked up. Kelly looked up as well. Although the ceiling appeared clean, she thought, "I wonder why he looked at the ceiling? I bet there was a leak there." He then looked down at the sink and said, "So, it would just be you?" "Yes sir, just me and my dogs." "What kind of dogs?" "Peeks" said Kelly. "Peeks?" He raised his eyebrows and looked over his glasses at her. "Yes sir, you know they are little dogs with smashed in faces, long hair and short legs. I really love this house she said smiling at Mr. Westbrook as she turned around to admire the kitchen. I have always loved old houses. It would be so much fun to decorate and would be perfect for me and my dogs. They really need a back yard to run in."

Mr. Westbrook was suddenly standing at the sink staring out the window. "Mr. Westbrook, said Kelly, what about this table and chairs, and the other things that are here, like the china, and the mirror and the bed upstairs?" Mr. Westbrook continued starring out the kitchen window and replied, "They were left here by the last owner. She was going to come back and get them but just never did. Then when it finally got time to close on the house she said we could just have them. They're yours if you want um. If you don't I can get rid of um. Louise said you're in the real estate business yourself. Who was your daddy?" "Yes sir," Kelly replied. "My parents owned Brown Real Estate. My father was Albert Brown. Both my parents were killed in a car accident last year. I'm running their business now." "I'm sorry to hear about your folks replied Mr. Westbrook. You look like the kind of young lady I would like to sell this house to. Being in real estate yourself you must have a good head on your shoulders and, you know what this house could sell for. Have you looked upstairs? The house has a large attic, I'll show you." As Kelly followed Mr. Westbrook to the living room he remarked, "This house is a restored historic landmark in this community, and the city. It is one of the most beautiful homes in Southside or in all of Birmingham for that matter. He laughed and said Louise says it would make a great bed n' breakfast but you can't get zoning in this area." They looked at all of the rooms upstairs as well as peeking into the attic. Afterwards Mr. Westbrook walked her to the front door.

"Here's my card, he announced. If you're really interested come by my office next week and we can discuss things more and maybe get the ball rolling. I might be willing to negotiate a little on the price for you but don't wait too long." Mr. Westbrook added "Did Louise tell you we're putting it on the market next week?" I won't have any problem getting what we ask for it. "Well, I am very interested and I'll get back with you next week" replied Kelly. "Well, feel free to look around all you want he said. I can leave the key under the mat for you if you think you want to look around again." "Thank you said Kelly that would be great. I might want to come by again tomorrow to take a second look." "Very well, he said I'll put the key under the mat. There you are he said as he bent down and put the key under the mat, just let me know." Mr. Westbrook said good-bye to Kelly and left her standing on the front porch.

She looked up and down the porch taking in the neighborhood scenery. She stood there for a few minutes this time feeling a little uncomfortable like the neighbors were watching her. Then she remembered seeing the man in the back yard. She had forgotten to mention him to Mr. Westbrook. She suddenly realized she had some other things to get done that afternoon but she felt tired and drained and had a headache so she decided to go home to rest and sleep on the idea of living in that house. She knew the key would be under the mat in case she wanted to come back the next day and look at it again. As she drove away from the house she glanced back one more time.

Kelly had decided she wanted to meditate about the house. She realized that this wasn't just a beautiful home that she happened to see in a picture but she had now become convinced that she had a premonition about this house in a dream. She asked herself should she commit to buying a house because she had a dream about it and might need to solve a mystery? Of course not! At this point she needed to doubt herself. Did she really dream about this particular house or just some house? The house was beautiful and exactly what she wanted that was for sure. So, by letting herself constantly harbor about a dream that wasn't making sense to her anyway shouldn't interfere with her buying the house if she really wanted it.

CHAPTER 14

Kelly had been determined not to dwell on the dream anymore. But it seemed no matter how hard she tried parts of the dream kept going through her head in her sleep and before long she was accepting that the dream and the house were somehow connected. She knew she had to follow it through. She wanted to find out, what was the meaning of this dream that she was compelled every night to dream about? In between the dream and during the day she would think more and more about how it would be to live in the house and she would try to put the dream out of her mind because she couldn't help but grow more excited thinking in reality how great it would be to buy it and live there and have a normal life.

.It was almost as though something would guide her to this house in her dreams. In her dream once she turned the key and entered the house she would start walking and searching for someone. It was not uncommon at all for her to have a dream and then only parts of the dream would come to pass. Her mind was set almost like a program. A vision, a premonition, or a dream would pass through her mind. She would see it and know that it would come to pass. Then it would be gone forever and she would welcome the next premonition. The difference was that this dream somehow gave her the feeling that it was designed for her alone, because the power that would contact her once she was asleep kept showing her the same dream that did not pass quickly but stayed in her mind for examination over and over again.

Somehow out of nowhere she felt she was being contacted by a mysterious force that was continually reaching out to her almost every night calling to her mind. There were also elements in the dream such as the key. She kept wondering about the message for her in the dream and someone searching for her in her dream to give her a key and to give her a message. Was that something the key to the house? She pondered; "Is the key in the dream the key that unlocks the door to this house? Is the message meant to be taken metaphorically and does the key to the house hold a secret that I am meant to find the answer to? By using this key do I find out who is trying to contact me to tell me something?

Is this someone looking for me because I can help them and is having the key the only way I can help them? Is there a secret? What is the secret and what is the message? Should I give credibility to this dream or should I ignore it? Why should I put myself in a position to try and solve a mystery when there is no mystery except the one I may have created myself? Do I have to actually buy this house and live in it in order to solve this mystery? I ask myself again, should I go on this journey to its conclusion or drop it and try to go on with my life? Can I live my life to the fullest without first solving this mystery? I feel I've lived my life ok up till now. I do like the house, but would I be making a mistake if I buy it? Or is my mind just facing a new type to challenge?"

Kelly had a restless weekend. She tossed and turned in bed and had reoccurring dreams about the house again. She had now only become more inquisitive and knew she wanted to return to the house and examine each room and try to get in touch with her inner feelings about why this was happening to her. By Monday morning the house had become a bee in her bonnet that she couldn't get rid of. She concluded that she needed to find some answers. While getting ready to go to the office she began thinking more seriously about buying that beautiful house. She thought about it all day at work and by the end of the day she was excited to see it again. She took off from work around 4:00 PM and headed back to Southside.

She carefully examined all of the rooms looking in the closets, at the floors, the windows, doors and locks. She was still uncertain that she should commit herself to buying an old house and living there by herself. When she really thought about it, it was kind of spooky but at the same time it had been restored so beautifully that she could imagine living there for the rest of her life. The design of it was unique and elegant. There was the staircase, the beautiful fire places, the original custom crown molding in all the rooms, the hardwood floors and of course the great columns. The second time she walked from room to room she felt much more at home in the surroundings. There were a few places in the house that did have a different feel. A time of two she found herself feeling very sad and she would try to shake off the feeling. Kelly wondered about the history of the house and all of the past owners. She would need to look at the deeds. She tried to forget about the dream and by Monday morning she thought she had made up her mind. She drove to Mr. Westbrook's office around lunch time to fill out a mortgage application.

Mr. Westbrook wasn't in his office but Kelly took the paper work from Marla his secretary and sat down at a large wooden table. When she had completed the application, she decided she would pick Marla's brain and find out if she had known the previous owner and ask her what she thought about her leaving the furniture behind. Marla said she didn't know the owners but just knew that the wife had moved out about five years or so ago and had left the furniture and had sold the house to Mr. Westbrook. Kelly remarked that it seemed strange that someone would leave such expensive looking furniture.

"Well, I guess replied Marla sometimes people do crazy things when they're under duress. Maybe the wife just didn't want the furniture after her husband died. Maybe those things reminded her too much of memories they had together." "Oh?" Kelly remarked. "I got the impression from Mr. Westbrook that just the one lady lived in the house." Marla replied "Did he say that?" "No" said Kelly. "He didn't say that exactly but he kept referring to the owner like there was just one owner." "Well, said Marla, she was the only owner after her husband died." "How did her husband die?" asked Kelly. "All I know said Marla is he was killed in some type of home accident. I think he died from a fall. That's why his wife sold the house and moved to Florida where some of her relatives lived.

I do know that's where she lived for a while before she moved back to Birmingham to take care of her mother. I think she met her husband in Florida too. They got married here and moved into that house after her mother died." "Wow, said Kelly this is a little unexpected. I didn't know about all of that." Then Kelly replied "Could you ask Mr. Westbrook to give me a call before you begin processing my application?" "I certainly will" she replied. Kelly left the office very perplexed. She couldn't believe that Mr. Westbrook had not mentioned that a married couple had owned the house and that the husband had died at the house. She had to know exactly what happened.

CHAPTER 15

The rest of the week was hectic as usual plus Kelly had to meet with the company accountant and family attorney. She also talked with Dan Carter who bought her father's agency in Atlanta about coming down to Birmingham to assist her with a few business matters at the office. It was the weekend before she knew it and Mr. Westbrook had not called her during the week. Saturday morning the phone rang around 9:00 AM. It was Mr. Westbrook. He apologized for not calling her before then and said he'd got her message but he had been so busy all week he didn't have the chance to return her call.

"I've got your application, he said. You must have decided on the house." Kelly told him she went by to see the house again and that she was pretty sure now that she wanted to buy it but was concerned about learning from Marla that one of the past owners had died in an accident at the house. Kelly said that it really bothered her when she found out about it and she wanted to know how this man had died. Mr. Westbrook said he would have discussed that with her if she had decided she really wanted to buy the house but didn't see any reason to bring it up at their first meeting. Kelly also knew from selling real estate herself that Mr. Westbrook might not have wanted to discuss the death of the previous owner if he thought it might hinder the sale of a house. Although from her experience in real estate, the death of a previous owner would not usually hinder the sale of a house if someone really wanted to buy it bad enough. What bothered

Kelly was that it became suddenly very clearly to her why she was having dreams about the house and why she had been more or less summoned to the house. It had something to do with the death of the owner. But what did that unfortunate circumstance have to do with her?

Mr. Westbrook said what happened was just a terrible unfortunate accident. He said the owner, Joe Hardy needed help putting a new roof on his house and Bill Saunders offered to help Joe the owner put the new roof on his house, when Joe lost his footing and fell. Joe died of a broken neck from the fall. Mr. Westbrook said "The police decided it was an accident and as far as I know, there was no real investigation." Mr. Westbrook said Joe Hardy had done several jobs for Bill and as a favor Bill was helping Joe put on a new roof at his house.

Mr. Westbrook also mentioned that Bill's nephew who had worked for him since he was a kid got to where he stayed out all night drinking and wouldn't show up for work half the time and Bill had heard Joe did good work so he hired him to do some roofing jobs. He told Kelly, "I am not saying you are irresponsible but you know how irresponsible some young people can be. Bill got tired of his nephew not showing up for work and fired him. Joe was a hard worker and he could rely on Joe and I think he had decided to put him on his payroll full time around the time the accident happened. In fact, I think Bill mentioned he was going to ask Joe to go into partnership with him.

Mr. Westbrook told Kelly again that the accident was very unfortunate but that kind of thing happens and that it shouldn't prevent her from buying the house if she really wants it. "I'll tell you what" he said, "Louise was good friends with Joe Hardy's wife Cindy and Cindy's mother. They use to attend our church. Why don't you call her if you have any questions or concerns about buying the house? We want you to be happy. It is your decision. Why don't you call her?" Kelly said she might give her a call later on that day and said she would get back with him.

About 7:00 pm that evening Kelly called Mrs. Westbrook. "Hi Louise, this is Kelly Brown." "Hi Kelly, how are you doing?" "Fine" she said. "Marvin said you saw the house. He said the way you went on when ya'll met that you really loved it. Do you think you're ready to buy or were you thinking you might want to keep looking for a while?" "Oh I love the house said Kelly and I was pretty sure I wanted to buy it. I guess he told you I had some concerns when I learned one of the owners had died at the house. He said you knew Cindy and her mother pretty well." Kelly rambled on "I can understand why the wife would have wanted to sell the house and move after her husband had died at his own home in a horrible accident. I don't know that I would have wanted to continue living there either. I guess that explains why she left some of the furniture pieces behind as well." Louise interrupted; "Are upset because someone died in the house?" Kelly gave a little laugh.

"Well yes, I am little upset because I had to learn about it from Mr. Westbrook's assistant. I feel that is the kind of information I think a homeowner should pass on to a potential home buyer. You know, I sell real estate to, and I would have to mention something like that to a new buyer. Kelly continued "You know some people might be sensitive to living in a house where someone passed, maybe not all but some would." Mrs. Westbrook in a poised manner cleared her throat and said, "Well Kelly, since you have been in real estate for many years yourself you must have seen times when home owners pass and their home goes up for sale. Unfortunately, sometimes folks die at home. It happens all the time. You seemed so excited about the house and buying your first home, and we wanted it for you. I guess neither one of us thought to discuss the past owners with you and well, of course at the time, we really didn't know for certain if you wanted to buy the house."

"To answer your question though, yes, I knew Cindy and her mother. They attended our church. Cindy and Joe lived in the house before we bought it. The house was actually Cindy's childhood home. She moved out about a year after Joe died. It was very sad and unfortunate the way he died. He was putting a new roof on the house and he slipped and fell off and the fall broke his neck. You know that roof has a real deep slant and goes straight down." "Was he putting the roof on by himself?" asked Kelly. "Bill Sanders who owns Saunders Roofing was helping him," she replied.

"Bill has worked for us for years. He does all of our roofing jobs and is a very reputable person. If you have any roofing or in fact any plumbing problems, I recommend him highly, he's very good." "You know," she added, "Bill was actually one of Cindy's childhood sweethearts. They went together in high school. Joe had started working some for Bill and as I understood from Marvin, there was a leak in the kitchen ceiling and it was time a new roof was put on anyway, so I believe Bill offered to help him with it. It was unfortunate that while they were tearing off the old roofing, I guess Joe just lost his footing and fell."

Mrs. Westbrook continued, "My daughter Faye who went to high school with Cindy said that after the accident Cindy was terribly depressed and just lost interest in the house. She moved back to Florida where she had been living with some of her mother's relatives before she met Joe. I don't know why she left those things in the house. She might have thought Faye could use them or maybe she didn't have room for them where is moved or maybe she decided she didn't want them. Anyway, Cindy mentioned to Fay that she was moving and was going to sell the house. That's how we came to buy it. Cindy knew Faye had always loved that house since she was a little girl. I can remember Faye would point at it when we drove by on our way to church and say, "Oh look, there's my house." "At the time said Louise, Faye had just gotten engaged and we were helping her look for a house. So, the house was available it seemed at a perfect time. But like I told you at the luncheon she and her so called fiancé never made it to the altar, so now, we need to sell it."

"So, Cindy was raised in the house?" asked Kelly. "Yes," said Louise. Christine and Jack bought the house I believe in the 1940's. They had Cindy right after. As I remember Christine had some female problems after Cindy was born so Cindy ended up being an only child. Jack died of a heart attack after Cindy went off to college. I can't remember where she attended but she had an aunt on her mother's side that lived in Pensacola and she attended college somewhere down there. Then her mother died in 1993 of breast cancer. Cindy then moved back in the house for awhile and then went back to Florida again. I think that's where she met Joe, at a Christian church event. They fell in love, and they moved here and were married and lived in the house until the accident. Louise went on, "Faye said Cindy loved the house and said that she and Joe were going to eventually restore it back to its original state. I know they worked real hard on the place. I know because sometimes we would drive by there on the weekends on our way to mall or church and they would be out in the yard working."

Kelly was listening but her mind kept drifting back to the fact that she was thinking about buying a house where a man had died from falling off the roof. Would she really be comfortable living in a house where that had occurred? All her life she had experienced psychic premonitions about things that would happen. Was the dream she kept reliving every time she entered the house and walked through the house connected to prior events that had occurred in that house? In the past Kelly had dreams and premonitions about living people. Had this reoccurring dream actually been about Joe? The house and the dream seemed so connected. Was Joe the man she saw in her dream who was searching for her to give her a key? But how could that be? Joe was deceased. Was she having dreams about a deceased man?

Kelly suddenly interrupted Louse with a question. "You said Bill Saunders and Cindy were high school sweethearts. Do you think Bill still had a thing for her when she moved back and married Joe?" "I don't think so replied Louise, not after she moved back here from Pensacola. That was just a high school crush. You know how kids are with their first love. When Cindy left after she graduated and went off to college she didn't see Bill for several years. I recall while she was gone Faye said she guessed Bill's crush was finally over because he had met this girl from Tuscaloosa and they had gotten engaged. Before they got married they were out at some park taking some pictures and she fell off a cliff and was killed. It came out later that she was married although she had told Bill she was divorced."

"Wow, said Kelly I was going to say that sometimes seeing someone again no matter how many years could re-kindle an old flame or if he still had hurt feelings he could have even felt revengeful." "Oh my Lord no, I don't think so," replied Louise. "Why I would never think of such a thing. If that was the case, why would Bill have hired Joe to work for him?" "Well, said Kelly, I guess you have a point." Although Kelly surmised that pretending to become friends with someone could be a ploy invented to mask a more sinister motive like a motive Saunders might have had to pretend he was friends with Joe in order to get close to Cindy again and at the same time have the opportunity to get revenge on the man who was preventing him from being with Cindy. Kelly continued, "Well Louise, I do love the house, and I really think it could be a new start for me there. It's been a year since I lost my parents and I'm desperately trying to get a new perspective on life. I am also in the process right now of selling their home and my townhouse. Is it ok if I let you know tomorrow?"

"Ok dear, said Louise that will be fine." Kelly stood up with the phone in her hand and tried to stretch her back. She said, "Well, I'd better let you go, it's getting late. I told myself I would start exercising again so I'd better head out to the track." "Ok dear," said Louise "I will talk with you in the morning. By the way what track do you go to?" she asked. Kelly replied, "When I run I go to the campus track. I just signed up to take some aerobic classes at the gym there as well." "Oh really," said Louise. "Faye has just started going to some exercise classes there too I believe. Maybe you'll see her there. We favor a lot so if you see her you would know who she is, like me, short with long brown hair." "Ok," said Kelly "I'll be sure to look for her when I go."

CHAPTER 16

Kelly was somewhat satisfied with the answers Louise had given her about Joe Hardy's death but maybe Louise didn't know everything. Kelly now had a suspicious and unsettled feeling about Joe Hardy's death. Sure accidents happen and even freak accidents like falling off a roof can happen. He could have just slipped and fell off the roof. But knowing now that there was a history between Bill Saunders and Cindy puts a different light on things. Kelly thought, "If I wasn't continuously haunted myself by this reoccurring dream I would just accept that Joe fell off the roof and let dead dogs lie so to speak. But the dream keeps bringing me back to the beginning where I am in a large house and someone is searching for me and trying to give me a key and a message." Her mind kept revisiting the part of the dream where she saw a man in the distance but she couldn't make out his face. Then there were two men standing together in a discussion. She wondered, "Who are the two men?"

Parts of the dream kept reoccurring to her. Her mind stayed cluttered with so many thoughts but more than anything else that one particular dream seemed to be totally consuming her thoughts every day and every night. She would wake up remembering she had been searching for someone. She had tried different doors to different rooms as she walked down a long hallway. Most of her premonition dreams came and went as a onetime event but this one had lingered on and on. Each time she had entered the house she would suddenly get the same déjà

vu feeling again and began remembering and experiencing parts of the dream again.

She had to wonder if Bill Saunders was still in love with Cindy and may have wanted to take revenge on her or her husband because he could never have her. She had to wonder, "Could he have been responsible for Joe Hardy's death?" "What about this married woman that Bill Saunders was dating that fell off a cliff? Was that really an accident? Had anyone tried to connect the dots?" She was curious and wanted more answers. She hoped she would run into Faye so she could pick her brain about Bill Saunders and Cindy's relationship. She had looked forward to going to the track that night but decided it was too late to go. She decided she would try and look for Faye the next time she went.

CHAPTER 17

Monday was a full day for Kelly and the beginning of another busy week. She had to make a decision about buying the house. She finally decided that even though there were unanswered questions in the back of her mind, so to speak, surrounding the death of the owner, the beauty of the house, and its enchantment and now even the growing mystery that surrounded the house entertained her mind and posed questions that she wanted to know the answers to. She wanted to solve this mystery that was reaching out to her from beyond her imagination and she really wanted that house, so she bought the Hardy House from the Westbrook's and began making preparations to move in at the end of the month. The following Thursday Kelly finally made it to the track and went to the campus building to attend an exercise warm up class.

The warm up classes lasted 30 minutes and then she planned she would walk or run on the track after that. She asked the lady at the front desk if Faye Westbrook was in that class. The lady glanced up at her and nodded in the direction of the back of the room. Kelly walked to the back and asked the small petite lady with long brown hair if she was Faye and she said she was. Kelly introduced herself as the lady who just bought the Hardy's house. Faye replied, "Oh, mother told me she sold it to you and that you were upset when you found out about Joe's death." "Well, a little" replied Kelly and said "I was shocked to find out the previous owner had died falling off the roof." "Your mother said you and Cindy Hardy are good friends and I've really thought about trying to contract her to see if she might have changed her mind and might want the things she left in the house before I get rid of them."

Of course that wasn't completely true but Kelly needed to start the conversation in some fashion. Faye replied, "Why don't we talk after the warm up class?" "Ok" said Kelly. After the exercise class was over Kelly caught up with Faye leaving for the track. As Kelly walked along beside her on the track, she began, "Like I said, I wanted to see if Cindy wants those items she left in the house before I give them away." Faye just kept looking straight ahead as she walked. Kelly went on; "I was a little upset when I heard about the owner dying at the house." "The way I found out was I was in your dad's office filling out a mortgage application and the lady in the office, what's her name? Anyway, she said the reason those things were left was because the wife might have been upset because her husband died in an accident at the home and she just wanted to move as soon as possible." "Your dad said this roofer; Bill Saunders, was helping Mr. Hardy put on the roof when he fell. Your mom also said that Cindy and Bill Saunders were once high school sweethearts."

For the first time, Faye looked over at Kelly and raised her eyebrows. "They were high school sweethearts?" Faye laughed and said "They only dated for a short time. He was an insane, crazy loony tune, fatal attraction asshole freak that stalked her and ruined her life in high school. Because of him she had to move out of town and hide at her aunt's house in Florida and start a new life there. She moved to Florida and I lost one of my best friends. He gave her nothing but grief her junior and senior year in school." "Really?" replied Kelly. Faye continued on, "At first things were ok and she really liked him. He was on the football team, she was a cheerleader, and then he started getting jealous. He started following her everywhere she went. He had to know where she was at all times and who she was with at all times. Any party she went to without him, he would show up and cause a scene and he would try and force her to leave with him. When she wouldn't go he would start yelling and calling her names. One time I saw him take her by the arm and jerk her so hard she cried out in pain.

She kept bruises on her wrists and arms. He use to drink a lot too. I don't know if he ever actually hit her but he still abused her physically and mentally. He would call her house in the middle of the night to make sure she was at home. Cindy was real popular in school and she was friendly with a lot of people including guys but I don't think she ever gave him a reason not to trust her. He was just insanely jealous and plain crazy. I remember one time he hid on her front porch and waited for her to come home to see who she was with and he also hid in the bushes. She could see his car parked from her bedroom window and she said sometimes he would sit out in his car all night and watch her house. Her parents finally had to get a restraining order on him and after that he mailed her a letter and said he was going to kill himself if she wouldn't see him. She finally got to where she couldn't take it any longer and after graduation she moved back to Florida to live with her aunt. I think she lived there until she graduated from college. I think she lived in Florida until her mother got sick."

Kelly said, "Wow, do you think he ever got over her?" "Well, said Faye, he's always dated a lot anyways, even when he was crazy about Cindy. He was always two-timing her. Anytime I see him now he is with some new girlfriend. The last I heard he had gotten involved with this married woman, and they became the talk of the town for awhile. They were on a secret date when she fell off a cliff at a water park and then it all came out that she was married. I guess he was over Cindy by then, but you never can tell. I think she was his only true love." Kelly thought to herself, that Bill Saunders had been either too immature to handle the relationship back then or he really had some mental issues and might still have some.

Kelly looked at Faye and exclaimed, "And he's the guy Cindy allowed to help her husband put a new roof on four stories up from the ground? "I don't think so!" Faye said, "My dad said that Bill and Joe had become friends. Dad told me and Mom that Joe had worked in construction and he was real smart with building things. I know Joe had done a few jobs for my dad but I think he was looking for steady work so my dad told him to call Bill. My dad uses Bill's company to do most of his roof and plumbing work. Anyway, I know Bill gave Joe some roofing jobs and of course he did find out Joe was married to Cindy so, I don't know what he thought. But you do know Bill was helping Joe put the roof on his own house when he fell? Faye asked." Kelly replied, "I know, you're Dad told me." Then Kelly said "I wonder how Cindy handled Joe and Bill being friends."

"Well, said Faye, Cindy's pretty much the type of person to let bygones be bygones. Even with all that happened in high school she's the type to forgive and move on. So, she may have thought it would be ok after all those years of not seeing each other, for Bill to help Joe with the roof. She probably thought that Bill had gotten over her by then and besides he could see she was now married and in love. She never mentioned to me that Bill was giving her any trouble after she moved back here and she and Joe got married. I guess things were ok, but l don't know for sure because she never said. Of course I've always thought Bill was crazy, a real butt because of the way he treated her and I still do. I know I personally wouldn't give him the time of day because he has always scared me. He had a reputation for having a bad temper when he was younger, and then that married woman dying the way she did, falling off of a cliff. If she made him mad enough he might have even pushed her off." "Do you think he could have pushed Joe off the roof?" ask Kelly. "Unless he's changed a lot, I could see him doing that," replied Faye. "Really?" asked Kelly.

"Well, Faye bounded, you know if he still had a thing for Cindy he might have thought, if I can't have her, no one can. He could have still been in love with her and insanely jealous of Joe, who knows. If you only knew Cindy you would understand Faye said. She was a wild child back then and she still is now. Cindy is really cute. She looks like a little barbee doll. She's a lot of fun, always the life of the party and can be a little bit of a flirt when she wants her way. I don't think she would have intentionally led Bill on but if she was being friendly again with him, he may have taken it the wrong way. Her flirting could give someone the wrong idea. Although I know, she loved Joe. You could tell when you saw them together and you could see he worshiped her."

Kelly and Faye finished their walk and standing at the campus track exit exchanged phone numbers with each other. Kelly thanked her, and they said quick goodbyes. Kelly's conversation with Faye had really given her something to think about on the drive back home. After learning some bare facts about Cindy, Joe and Bill Saunders from Faye she actually felt a little more at ease about moving into the house. She wanted to know more about Bill Saunders and wondered how she could come up with a plan to meet him. Maybe if I talk to him about the accident I could clear up some of the mystery about the dream. "Somehow, she thought, he must have had something to do with Joe Hardy's death and I've got to talk to him." She pondered, "This is crazy. Why am I stuck in the middle of this?"

She concluded that there was someone or something trying to reach out to her in her dreams. Is it Joe Hardy? She knew she had to get some questions in her mind resolved about the dream and the house before she could have some piece of mind. The next day after some much needed sleep she awoke feeling excited about moving into her new home and looked forward to finally selling her townhouse.

CHAPTER 18

It was now the end of October and almost a year had gone by since Kelly's parents had passed away. She had decided to throw herself into packing, cleaning and moving into the house by the end of November and not to worry about decorating for Christmas that year. She called Betty Cartel of Cartel Interiors and discussed a few decorating ideas for spring. Kelly made an appointment with Betty to come over after Christmas. Kelly moved as she planned and before she realized it Christmas had come and gone and New Year resolutions that she always made had never crossed her mind.

She had been working ardently cleaning and decorating her new home while still having to keep some long hours at the office. By the first week of January she was totally exhausted. It wasn't until February before she felt somewhat settled in. She was relaxing one evening on the couch that was positioned in front of the fireplace in the living room. She was snuggled with a velour throw and a glass of wine. Her dogs were lying at her feet in front of the fireplace. Wow, she thought finally, this is really nice. She lay back on the couch pillow and starred up at the high ceiling. Her eyes slowly following the lines of white crown molding down each side of the ceiling until it met in the corners of the wall. "This house is so big and so quiet she thought. I love it."

"Oh man," she said aloud while glancing at her dogs lying beside the couch. "It's almost eleven o'clock girls, I'll never be able to get up at five tomorrow." She reluctantly jumped up from the warm spot on the couch and walked quickly to the kitchen in her sock feet. "Come on girls, let's go out back so I can get to bed." They ran behind her, the littlest one Abby hitting the back door with her paws. She flipped up the back yard light switch and let them out. She stood in the doorway and watched them run out on the cold wet grass to take a tinkle and then scurry back up the back steps. After locking the back door, she checked the basement door.

Just one more check she thought as she opened the sunroom door, switched the light on, looked around and turned the light off and closed the door. She walked back through the living room and turned the lamps off in the living room and checked the front door lock. She switched on the upstairs hall light from the bottom of the stairs and swooped up Abby in her arms. She climbed the stairs as her big dog Chloe followed them. When she reached the top of the stairs she flipped the light switch down turning the upstairs hall light off. She got into bed and lay there a few minutes getting nestled in. "Good night little ones" she said and turned the bedside lamp off.

It seemed like she had just finally gotten to sleep when she was suddenly awakened by what sounded like pots and pans clanging on the floor in the kitchen. She quickly jumped out of bed. "Oh my god, she thought, what if someone has broken in." Her dogs began barking loudly as she ran to the bedroom door. She stood still for a moment and listening for more sounds. Then she flipped on the overhead light and walked to the bedside table and took out her revolver. With the gun in hand she quietly opened the door and stepped out into the hallway. She slowly closed the bedroom door behind her while her dogs continued to bark loudly. She was startled because the upstairs hallway light was on and she knew she had turned it off before going to bed. "My god, she thought, someone is in this house." She suddenly felt her face getting hot. She could hear her heart beating loudly in her chest. Her ears felt hot and her temples were pulsating. She was suddenly sick with fear as her stomach turned over and she felt jittery all over.

Her body was shaking so badly that she couldn't control it. She began what seemed like an endless journey down the stairs holding the gun with both hands in front of her. She remembered what a police officer had once advised her after she had been flashed by a man near her office. It was after that close encounter including another with a peeping Tom that she finally decided to purchase a gun for protection. The police officer had told her; "Remember, you know how to shoot this gun so be confident, hold it steady and don't be afraid to use it, but do not point it at an intruder unless you intend to use it because a man like myself could easily take it from you and use it on you first." She remembered his advice and held the gun firmly but still felt helpless and powerless as she started down the old wooden staircase that creaked with every step she took.

When she reached the bottom of the staircase, she switched on the living room light. There was no one there. She knew the sounds had come from the kitchen and if someone was in there, they could see her outline as she approached the kitchen. She felt like a sitting duck and suddenly became very angry that someone could do this to her in her own home. She held the gun with her right hand and stormed to the kitchen doorway reached in and flipped up the light switch. The kitchen was icy cold. She shivered as she felt a cold breeze engulf her. The kitchen cabinets that lined the right side of the wall were trembling and the china inside the cabinet was making a high pitched tinkling sound inside the cabinet. The glass in the back door was clanging and even the thick heavy door itself seemed to be trembling. She starred at the door in disbelief. As she took a step towards the door, the trembling sounds suddenly stopped and there was dead quiet.

She looked around the room. On the floor beside the chopping block lay her copper bottom frying pan and four pots. She had hung them over the chopping block on the large pot rack that hung from the ceiling. The rack was gently swaying back and forth making a squeaking sound that resembled a circus trapeze bar without the acrobat. As she stared at it, it swayed less and less and within only a moment before her eyes came to a complete stop. She glanced up at the ceiling. The rack looked bolted and secured in place. The site of the swinging rack sent chills up her back and she couldn't move. It was as though a hand had reached out and stopped the rack from swinging. She was being traumatized not only by what she was experiencing but by what she was sensing around her.

She felt overpowered. Her body felt heavy all over as she tried but couldn't move her arms or legs from the spot where she stood. She then realized her right hand was hurting from holding the gun so tight. She suddenly came to her senses and was able to take a breath and was about to leave the kitchen when she heard voices and walking over her head. It sounded like it was coming from upstairs somewhere, either from the above bed room or the attic. She ran out of the kitchen leaving the light on. She stood in the living room looking up at the staircase and listening for more footsteps but the voices and walking had stopped. She couldn't rationalize what had just happened to her.

There wasn't a logical explanation why the pots had fallen or what had caused the rack to swing enough to make the pots fall and what about the trembling cabinets and back door? She turned all the lights on downstairs and checked all the windows and all the rooms and in the closets downstairs. It was around 3:00 AM. When she reached the top of the stairs she glanced into the bedroom to the left and switched the light on. She slowly walked over to the closet and opened the door. She let out a sigh of relief. She checked the other rooms and returned to her bedroom and laid the gun on the bedside table. She turned on the overhead light as well as the bedside light. She lay there for awhile trying to listen for any sounds and eventually drifted back to sleep.

The next morning she took another look around in the kitchen. All seemed normal. The only explanation that she could come up with was that maybe there might have been a light earthquake. But it was so strange because the kitchen seemed to be the only room that was affected. She thought that maybe the walking sounds she heard could actually be some animal that might be up in the attic, but what about the voices? She couldn't explain away the voices she heard. She remembered the first day she looked at the house. She remembered that the dishes in the china cabinet seemed to be slightly trembling then. She had also felt a cold breeze in the kitchen that day. That was also when she had seen that man in the back yard. An earthquake seemed too bizarre she thought, but she would check the news when she got to work that morning.

As usual she was in a frantic rush to get to work that Friday. As she was about to enter the Brown Real Estate building, she decided to grab a newspaper from the news stand that Mr. Zeke ran down the street. She could see from the corner of her eye that someone was looking her way. Across the street was a very nice looking guy. She thought he looked about her age. He was about six feet tall, nice build, with dark hair, and had a nice tan. She concluded for that time of the year, he must have an outside job. He was smoking a cigarette and standing close to the corner street lamp. Kelly acknowledged he was looking at her by glancing his way and smiling. He nodded at her but didn't smile. Feeling nervous from his stare she flung her head back and glanced at him again but by then she could see he was too busy inhaling his last puff of smoke and flipping his cigarette butt into the street to notice.

She held the newspaper in her arms, secured her shoulder strap purse and turned and entered the Brown building. After she was inside and put her purse down she glanced across the street but he was gone. "Yep," "that's my luck" she said laughing, as she glanced over at Kim who must have had her mind on something else. Kelly hurried down the hall to the break room singing

"There Goes My Baby" while she poured a cup of coffee. When she returned she began talking to Kim. "All the good looking ones get away, and he was a good one who might have had some potential. But now he'll never know what a great and wonderful person he could have met. But, "who cares" she said. "I don't like a smoker anyway." "What are you talking about said Kim?" Kelly heard her but she had already switched her mind over to "work mode" and just replied back to her "oh nothing, good morning." "Good morning," said Kim.

Kelly said, "I bought a paper because I had a really weird thing happen last night at my house. I wanted to check to see if we had like a small earthquake or some kind of tremor last night. It was so weird. I woke up about 3:00 this morning. I heard a crash downstairs and it scared me to death. I thought someone had broken in. I went downstairs to check and some pots had fallen off the pot rack in the kitchen and the dishes in the cabinet were shaking." "Wow" Kim replied. "I don't think we had an earthquake. We don't have earthquakes in Alabama do we? At least I've never heard of one here, but I guess it's possible. I'll tell you one thing she said, I would be afraid to live in that big house by myself. You need a good alarm system installed." "I know" said Kelly. "That house is really big. If someone did break in, by the time I could get downstairs they would be gone." "Or they could hide and be waiting on you to come downstairs" said Kim. "Or they could come in downstairs and be upstairs and in my face before I could do anything about it" said Kelly. "You know," replied Kelly, "I think I will try and take a couple of days off next week. I need to call an alarm company to come out there and I also need to start cleaning out the attic.

And to top it off with all the other craziness, I could have sworn I also heard walking up in the attic and voices. The sounds must have been coming from outside but it really spooked me. I need some free time to look around up there and I'm not going to go up there at night. There are also a lot of boxes up there that I need to go through." At the end of the day Kim asked Kelly if she would like to go to a budget movie Saturday afternoon. This one was a James Bond movie. Kelly didn't really like that type of movie but agreed to go because she knew Kim would be disappointed if she couldn't go with her and she knew Kim wouldn't go by herself. So, as a favor Kelly said she would go. "Ok" said Kelly, I'm in. "After last night I need some double-o-seven."

CHAPTER 19

aturday morning Kelly found herself sleeping late for once
in a long time. When she finally got up and stirred around it
started to rain. The sound of the rain eased her mind and she
felt rested for a change. She stood in the kitchen and stared out
the back door window. She watched the rain falling gently on the
frozen ground in the back yard. It was the first week in February.
She had been in her new house a little over three months. She
took a deep breath and ran her fingers alongside the white lacy
curtain that hung on the window of the back door. She was in
deep thought about the guy she had seen downtown that Friday.
She couldn't help it. She had always been a hopeless romantic.
She could still see the tall dark haired stranger leaning against the
street lamp taking a draw from his cigarette while watching her.
As she turned her head his way their eyes met. She remembered
his quiet concentrated stare. His eyes seemed to be piercing
her right to the very core of her being. Her heart sank. Well, it
didn't happen quite like that she thought but it was a moment
she wouldn't forget for awhile and anyway, every time she thinks
about him it gets better. She wondered, "Why can't I ever meet
a really nice guy? Men, their all the same. If their good looking
their stuck on themselves and if they look like crap their still
stuck on themselves. Their all selfish and they all cheat but us
women continue to dream and open ourselves up to the same old
hurts over and over again." Kelly accepted that she was a hopeless
dreamer, a devout romantic and was certain she would always
remain one.

She thought back briefly about a couple of guys she had dated in college. John came to her mind. He lived in one of the townhouses on the same street where Kelly use to live. He was a family law attorney. He conducted his business from his home where he would meet with his clients and then conclude business at the courthouse. He was a colorful conversationalist when it came to law or politics but by her standards a lousy lover. Kelly had met him through Carol a college classmate. John had been Carol's divorce attorney. At first Kelly really liked his sense of humor but could tell from the beginning their relationship was headed for nowhere.

Kelly had not laid down any ground rules when they started seeing each other. She actually didn't think she had to, but before she knew what was happening he had designed his on ground rules that she found herself following. He also had boundaries that he stood guard over very well. Since they both worked downtown, he suggested that they meet for lunch every day at his special restaurant which was at a convenient time for him and at a convenient location but it wasn't really convenient for Kelly at all. His plan was that after work they would meet at his apartment for a drink and to conclude with a quickie before he finalized his paperwork. These weekly encounters soon became routine.

The relationship never graduated to a higher level. There was no romance. It was basically a situation designed as a convenience for his on-the-go ego life style. Eventually, Kelly blamed herself for feeling used. To be honest, she realized that maybe subconsciously she preferred having that type of relationship with him since she knew it was useless to expect she could have anything more with him. Maybe she was just lonely. Maybe he was too. Eventually she got tired of playing his silly routine game that had gone on for almost a year. What a shame Kelly thought. He was so good looking and was a really funny guy when they met. But she kept waiting for the Grand Finale in bed and that just never happened. After a while she decided to set her sights on someone else and started making up excuses not to see him. He still called her for a long time and he seemed very content to just engage in small talk about how his day had been the weather, his cases, and courthouse politics.

CHAPTER 20

Kelly escaped from her day dreaming and decided to get back to her plan of doing a thorough sanitize cleaning of the house, but finally came to the conclusion that it was turning out to be too much of a endless ordeal in which trying to get rid of the old musty moldy smells that lurked in the closets and cabinets was only going to be remedied by a new coat of paint to camouflage the smells. She decided to quit, take a shower and meet Kim at the mall to have lunch and take in that dreaded budget movie. That afternoon when she returned she fed and walked her dogs. It had continued to rain off and on all day and the temperature had only climbed in the forties. In the summer she was use to taking her dogs on walks on a jogging trail near her townhouse but since she had moved to the new house there was only the back yard and the alley for them to do their business in. Now of course it was February and in the dead of winter and it was cold and usually dark by the time she got home from the office.

That afternoon she walked her dogs on her usual inspection tour, out the front door, across the front yard around the side of the house and into the back yard, out through the back fence and down the alley. For the most part the neighborhood was quiet and peaceful and while she really didn't anticipate summer time that would bring out all the lawn mowers and neighborhood kids she guessed it still would be a true indication that the neighborhood had been hiding some sort of human life.

81

Since the driveway was in the back of the house, she had gotten into the habit of using the back door as the main entrance. After walking her dogs she headed back up the alley to the back of the house and latched the drive way fence behind her. She hurried them quickly into the house. Giggling she said, "Come on girls let's go in and get warm." She got undressed put her PJ's on and turned up the heat. She had gotten busy fixing a snack and watching TV when she realized she hadn't taken the trash out yet. She glanced at the kitchen clock. She couldn't believe it was a quarter past 10:00 PM. She thought she'd just run out real fast and take the trash and wouldn't bother putting on her jacket. She opened the back door, leaving it cracked a few inches.

She ran down the back stairs with bags in both hands letting the back storm door slam behind her. The light bulb at the back door had blown out. She had written light bulbs on her grocery list but hadn't bought them yet. Without the lighting from the back door light, there was very little light to see by in the back yard. It was barely illuminated by the alley street light that was located on the opposite side of the alley near the back drive gate. The grass looked wet and slippery as it glistened from the day's rain. The weather man's forecast had said freezing rain for overnight. The temperature had dropped into the 30's and ground was starting to freeze. As Kelly walked quickly towards the gate the wind cut through her thin flannel pajamas, her face and hands had become ice cold as she hurried down the driveway and opened the gate.

The trash can was on the outside of the gate. She tugged hard to remove the lid and dropped the trash in the can. As she replaced the lid she heard a sound behind her. She turned quickly to the sound. She jumped a little and gasped out loud putting her hand to her chest. She could see a man standing underneath the tree across the alley close to the street light. Although she couldn't see his face she knew it was a man because she could plainly see his outline. He was at least six feet tall; medium built and wore a heavy ski type jacket. The sound she had heard was him flicking his lighter open to light a cigarette.

She was suddenly filled with fear. The only thing she could think of was to run but that almost seemed silly. What if this was just some high school kid from the neighborhood hiding there to smoke? It had to be. Why would any normal person be standing out of sight under a tree in an alley at 10:00 PM at night in 30 degree weather? She wasn't waiting around to find out. She turned and reached for the gate latch that was raised in an upward position. It creaked as she pulled on it. Her fingers hurt and felt frozen. Her steps were stiff and awkward from the cold. She didn't want to think that this man might lung on her at any moment but thoughts ran through her head. "He might try and force himself in the house." She quickly moved inside the gate and pulled the latch down. Now she was going to run because she was freezing. She heard more movement behind her but she didn't look back. She turned quickly towards the house running lightly and swiftly on her tip toes. Her stiff erected body felt numb as she gazelled across the yard. In her mind's eye somewhere in time she was a tiny fairy, her thin but sturdy wings caring her to safety as they propelled her upward and away safely to her destination. She would soon be free, leaving the intruder far behind. Her long swirling hair was lifted up high by the cold night breeze while her long frail limbs carried her along with ingenuous speed. Yes, he had seen her and her beauty which was truly unmistakable but she was gone now forever, far from his grasp.

She couldn't let herself think that the sound she heard was him right behind her. "Let it be the sound of my pounding heart" she screamed to herself. She never looked back and upon reaching the back door parted it with her body and shut it hard behind her and quickly turned the dead bolt. She moved away from the kitchen door. She was inside but she still didn't feel safe. She could feel him on the outside of the house. His power and strength had suddenly gained momentum over her presence although she knew at that moment she was safe from harm. She was having a panic attack. She could picture him standing on the outside of the house. She was behind locked doors but still felt terrified. She couldn't stop trembling. Her face, ears and her entire body were on fire. She could hear her heart beating loudly. She stood at the back door listening for any sounds but there was none. She turned off the kitchen light and looked out the back door curtain to the alley. She couldn't see any movement. Everything looked quite and still. She searched the back yard with an investigating eye looking left then right for the man in the alley.

He was probably some high school kid now on his way home, walking down the alley laughing at how scared he had made her. But what if it wasn't some kid? What if someone was there planning on breaking in and she happened to have taken the trash out and discovered him? After all, this house had been vacant a couple of years and he was standing right in the alley directly across from the house. He might be some homeless person who knows how to get in the house maybe by the basement door and may have even slept in the house before. What if the man in the alley was the man she had seen in the back yard before she moved in? Maybe he was the one who had broken into the house and turned the hall lights on and knocked the pots off the rack and then left. Maybe it was him planning to terrorize me again.

But that doesn't make any sense. She turned the kitchen light back on and walked to the basement door to check the lock. The door was locked. She couldn't remember if she had left the outside basement door open although there was nothing she could do about it now. He could be in the basement and if he was in the basement he could break into the house from the upstairs basement door. If he was in the house she was a sitting duck she thought. From day one of moving in she had utilized the basement to store furniture, tools and anything she didn't really know what to do with. It was much easier at that time than trying to store things in the attic. But while moving things in an out she had forgotten several times to lock the downstairs basement door. She suddenly thought of the front door.

She rushed to the living room to check the front door, her dogs running at her heels like she was playing a game. She checked the lock and turned on the front porch light afraid but still hoping to catch the intruder standing there. She turned the light off and starred a minute out the front door window for movement in the yard. This experience had really rattled her. Although Kelly was very tired she was almost afraid to go upstairs to bed. What if he tries to break in while she was asleep? What if whoever that was in the back yard that day has a key? She had decided to call Mr. Westbrook Monday morning and tell him what had happened and ask him if he knows who the man in the back yard could have been. Kelly left the kitchen light on and a lamp in the living room on and went to bed. She carefully checked the bedrooms before going to bed. She placed her gun in her night stand and after awhile she finally was able to drift off to sleep.

CHAPTER 21

The next day was Sunday. She was up early and let her dogs out into the back yard and did a little investigating. The ground had been moist from the rain the night before although it was now frozen. She looked for cigarette butts or frozen foot prints in the back yard and underneath the windows but saw nothing. She took her dogs with her out to the alley and walked up and down and looked around the tree where the man had been standing. She was a little puzzled because there were no cigarette butts at all in that area. She knew freezing rain was still probable in the forecast for the late afternoon. Around 4:00 PM she was standing at the kitchen window when she heard the rain start. Rain drops begin to hit gently on the back door window pane. She went to the back door window and looked out. Her heart sank. There was that man again. He was standing beside the myrtle tree facing the back of the house. It was the same man she had seen in the back yard the first day she looked at the house. It was him, same face, and same clothes. He was standing very still, looking up at something on the roof.

He just stood there and didn't blink or move. He had a solemn and sad look on his face. He seemed far away in deep thought. Kelly was mesmerized by him. He looks so strange she thought. His skin is so pale and ashy looking. He didn't seem to notice her although she had the curtain pulled back and was looking at him from the window. All of a sudden the sky fell out and it started to rain much harder. He just stood there and didn't blink or budge. Kelly decided to confront him. She closed the curtain and opened the back door. "Hey," she called out as she opened the door, but he was nowhere in sight. It was raining harder now. She ran out into the back yard and looked both ways. "This is crazy" she said aloud, "hey you" she called as she ran around the house to the front yard but he was still nowhere in sight. She peered across the street to see if he had gone into another yard. She began running. She ran down the sidewalk in pouring rain looking both ways until she reached the end of the block.

That is just too weird she thought as she ran back to the house and entered through the back door. While she stood in the kitchen soaking wet and out of breath, the phone began to ring. The sudden sound of the phone ringing made her jump nervously. It was Kim from the office. "Hey," Kim said, "I forgot to tell you Saturday that Friday afternoon I got those two contracts you needed drawn up for you so, no worries Monday they will be ready." "Ok," that's great, replied Kelly. "We'll take care of those Monday." Then Kelly replied, "I meant to ask you yesterday when you could come over to see my haunted house." Kim laughed and said, "Is it haunted?" "Well," said Kelly, "you know a couple of weird things have happened since I moved in." "What kind of things asked Kim?" "Where do I begin?" said Kelly. "I told you about the night I woke up and the lights were on in the hall upstairs and the pots and pans had fallen off the pot hanger in the kitchen?" "Yes" replied Kim and you thought there might have been an earth quake." "Yeah", said Kelly. "Well, now I keep seeing this creepy man in my back yard. I just saw him again a few minutes ago. Then last night there was some man standing in the alley underneath a tree smoking a cigarette when I took the trash out.

He scared the crap out of me. It might even be the same man I told you I saw in my back yard. I had to run for my life back to the house. I was afraid he was going to break in." "Do you think you need to call the police?" Kim asked. "I don't know" said Kelly. "If anything else happens I will. Right now I am pretty stressed out and on top of that, I'm having this weird dream over and over about this house and I'm stressed over that as well." Kim replied "If I were you I would report it just to be safe and try to take your trash out while its daylight and keep your doors locked and the curtains drawn. I think I can come over tomorrow after work for a while if that's ok. I'll ask Jimmy tonight and see if it's ok with him. I don't think he has anything planed. He'll have to watch Mandy until I get home." "Ok, just let me know tomorrow" replied Kelly. Monday started off busy as usual. Kelly called Mr. Westbrook's office around 9:00 AM but got his voice mail. She decided not to leave a message and just to try him later.

Tuesday at lunch, Kelly decided to run over to Valley Antiques and see if she could find some vases to go on her living room mantel to set beside the beautiful old mirror that had been left above the fire place. She entered the store and made her way back to the section where the vases, dishes and lamps were located. She loved the English blue and white patterned dishes and blue cobalt glass ware. Her couch was baby blue velvet. She had planned to use a variety of blues, white, and yellows in the living room and in the kitchen. She spotted two tall cobalt blue swirled glass vases on a dresser. "These will be perfect," she thought. She checked them for cracks and chips. They were seventy nine dollars each. Kelly thought, just old retro vases, not worth much, but they will still look great on the mantel.

Kim said Jimmy would watch Mandy and that she would be right over after work. Kelly left about an hour early so she could go by the health store and pick up some herbal tea for her and Kim. When she got home she laid out the tea and cups and unwrapped the two vases she had bought earlier that day. She placed each vase on mantel, and then stood back to see if she had placed them an equal distance from the mirror. She returned to the kitchen to see Kim standing at the back door.

"Hi! Come on in" said Kelly. "Wow!" exclaimed Kim. "This house is so great, and your kitchen is huge!" "Yeah" said Kelly while glancing up at the high kitchen ceiling and nodding her head up and down agreeing, "it is huge." "That's one reason I love it she said. I love the tall ceilings and there's a lot of open space." "This table," Kim asked, "is it an antique?" "I'm not sure replied Kelly. It looks really old, but it's still in good shape. It sort of came with the house. The previous owner left it here along with those dishes in the cabinet. She also left a Queen Ann style bed that was up in the master bedroom. I took it down and put it in the basement. You and Jimmy are welcome to it if you'd like to take a look. The lady that lived her also left a beautiful beveled mirror that's hanging over the fire place. I'll show you in just a minute. I bought us some tea." "Hot tea sounds good," said Kim. "Great," said Kelly and she put the water on to boil.

"Talking about antiques," said Kelly "you won't believe what I found today at Valley Antiques. I found two beautiful cobalt blue vases for the living room mantel." "Come on" she said, "You've got to see these vases and the mirror I told you about." Before they could reach the living room, they heard a loud crash. Kelly went running into the room. One of the vases lay broken on the hearth. She just stared down in disbelief. "I can't believe this" she said. "How could it have fallen off?" "Where did you have it sitting" asked Kim. Kelly replied, "When I got in today I placed both vases on the mantel equally apart from the mirror and I know I put both of them far enough back on the mantel that they shouldn't have fallen off. Or maybe I didn't, said Kelly shaking her head. I'll tell you, I'm beginning to just not know anymore." "Well, said Kim in a sympathetic voice, maybe the antique store has another one like it or similar to it. It wouldn't have to match perfectly to look good. You know this house is very old. Maybe the shutting of the back door when I came in jarred the vase and caused it to fall." "Yeah, maybe your right," said Kelly as she stooped down to pick up the broken glass. "I'll just look for another one, maybe tomorrow."

Kim said "I hear the water boiling. I'll make the tea." She took off to the kitchen. Kelly stood up and touched the mantel with her fingers still pondering on how the vase had suddenly fallen. Kelly muttered to herself, "How could that have happened, I know I had the vase secured on the mantel." She looked at the other vase on the far side of the mirror. The bottom was fairly heavy so to her there wasn't really a logical explanation to what made the vase fall.

CHAPTER 22

It was the end of the week before she knew it and business had become a little slower so Kelly had decided to start closing the office at 4:00 PM on Fridays. She had returned home and decided to start on a project she had not been anticipating. She needed to go through the rest of the boxes she had stored in the left front upstairs bedroom. She was sorting through some of the boxes when she began to hear the sound of dripping water. The sound seemed to be coming from above her. She could hear it clearly. It sounded almost like how dripping would sound if it echoed in a cave or like the plop, plop sound of water dropping down into a well.

She looked up and checked the bedroom ceiling. She looked in the closet and also in the fireplace to see if she could see anything wet. Everything looked dry in those places. Where was the sound coming from? No, don't tell me she thought, that all this rain has caused a leak. She listened again. She walked into the hall and stood quietly listening while looking up at the ceiling. The ceiling in the hall looked dry but she did seem to hear the sound more distinctly in the hall and concluded that the leak might be in the attic. She had only briefly looked in the attic when she first saw the house with Mr. Westbrook. "Well, she thought, if there is a leak I've got to try and find out where it is coming from. If I can't find it, eventually it could run me into a lot of money. I should have checked better for any leaks when we were looking up there."

She ran downstairs and got the flashlight from the kitchen cabinet drawer and ran back upstairs. Getting the attic ladder down was the killer. She tugged hard till it finally gave way and she pulled it down to the floor exposing the attic opening. She could see from below the attic had good light. "Here goes nothing," she said in a low voice. She climbed the twelve tiny rickety stairs to the top. She turned on the flash light while still perched on the ladder and shinned it around in the room. She boosted herself up onto the attic floor and looked around as the heat and musty smell hit her in the face. To her amazement the back of the attic had a good amount of light coming in from the large back window that centered the room and faced the back yard. As she began to walk around she could hear the dripping more clearly. "Ah ha!" She said aloud, "it's coming from over there." She was headed to the opposite wall when she stopped and glanced out the window.

The dripping noise suddenly stopped. She starred down to the back yard. "Wow, she thought this must be what that man in the yard is starring at; the attic window." She stood there for a moment in a daze, her eyes were fixed on the spot by the myrtle tree where she had seen him twice before. Then, from the corner of her eye she saw something shiny. She glanced down and saw a flat piece of silver metal wedged between the floor and the wall underneath the edge of the window. She tugged on it until she pulled it out. "This looks like a crowbar or maybe some kind of tool used to do roofing or to change a tire, and that looks like blood." She looked more closely at the forked end of the medal bar. "Someone must have killed a rat or something up here with it." She looked around in the attic.

She noticed that the dripping had stopped. As she glanced around, except for the spider webs the ceiling looked dry and she couldn't see any places where the walls or floor were wet. There were several old boxes pushed up against the far wall that were closed up and stacked neatly together that also appeared dry from the outside. She thought the best thing to do at some point would be to drag them to the attic opening and pull them down the stairs. That way she could look through each box and then call a thrift store to pick them up. But she would do that another day since it was getting dark. The dripping sounds had stopped and until it started again she wasn't going to look any further. And since it was getting dark, she wanted to get down from the attic. She took the crowbar with her down to the kitchen and put it under the sink, planning to take it down to the basement later on.

CHAPTER 23

That night she was at the kitchen sink when she felt something wet drip on her hand. She quickly pulled back her hand and glanced up at the ceiling above the sink. The ceiling was circled with brownish red stains. There was a red glob of goo that sat in the middle of the stain. Suddenly she felt another drop hit her hand that she had placed back on the edge of the sink. She looked down at her hand and jumped back from the sink. "The circles on the ceiling look like watered down blood," she thought. "Oh my god, something must have died up there because that looks too much like blood." She washed off her hand and pulled out a bucket from under the sink. She knew she had to find out where the leak was coming from. She suddenly heard footsteps in the attic. It sounded like someone walking across the floor. Then the walking changed to a shuffling sound. Then there were sounds like something heavy was crashing against the wall and the sound of something falling.

Kelly stood very still and listened but just like the elusive dripping sounds the footsteps and shuffling sounds stopped as suddenly as they started. She went to the living room and stood at the bottom of the stairs and listened but heard nothing. She climbed the stairs and turned on the light in the left front bedroom. All was quiet in there. She walked down the hall to bathroom and to the next bedroom. All was quiet and undisturbed in those rooms as well. She went back down to the kitchen and looked up at the kitchen ceiling again. The spot she saw looked larger than before.

"I guess I will call Bill Saunders tomorrow, thought Kelly. I had been trying to think of a way I could meet him and ask him some questions about Joe Hardy's accident. Now I have a good reason to call him since he put this roof on and it is still under warranty. Mr. Westbrook gave me his card and I have it in my purse. I will call him in the morning about the ceiling." She remembered what Faye had implied during their conversation. Faye thought there was a possibility that Saunders might have killed Joe to either get revenge on Cindy or to get rid of Joe so that he would have a second chance with Cindy. Funny, she thought, I remember Mr. Westbrook saying it had all started with a leak in the kitchen ceiling. If there hadn't been a leak in the kitchen ceiling and Joe hadn't wanted to repair the leak, which eventually lead to replacing the roof, would he be dead right now?

Did Joe Hardy ask Saunders to help him repair the leak and they decided to go ahead and put a new roof on? What if Saunders's had planned all along to act like he was going to help Joe in order to kill him and push him off the roof? She stared up at the spot again wondering if this leak was in the same place as the old leak was. This could be the original leak and might not have ever been repaired the day Joe fell off the roof. Kelly felt she was jumping to conclusions and worrying too much about a simple leak and how Bill Saunders was involved with what had happened to Joe.

She assured herself the leak would be repaired but she still had an uncomfortable feeling that she could not shake and walked in and out of the kitchen the rest the evening starring up at the ceiling as the spot seemed to grow larger. She placed another bucket beside the sink and listened to the loud dripping sounds as each drop of nasty red brown liquid hit the bottom of the buckets. "Oh why did I buy this place she mumbled? Why couldn't I have settled for a cute little garden home? I have probably gotten myself into a real mess."

CHAPTER 24

The next morning around 8:00 AM Kelly called Mr. Saunders's office. "Hello" someone said into the phone. Kelly replied, "May I speak to Mr. Saunders?" A man replied, "This is he." Kelly continued, "Yes sir, my name is Kelly Brown. I just bought a house from Marvin Westbrook". "Yes mam!" He replied. "Yes sir, she said, he told me your company put the roof on this house. I'm trying to get settled in here but there's a leak in the kitchen ceiling." "Well mam, do you know when we put the roof on?" "Mr. Westbrook said it was about five years ago, said Kelly. It's the big white Colonial home on Magnolia Street in Southside. Do you remember?" "Yes mam, he said slowly. It's the Hardy house." "Yes sir," she replied. "They lived her before Mr. Westbrook bought it. Mr. Westbrook said I should call you if I had any problems with the roof leaking." "Well, what kind of problem are you having" he asked. "I have been hearing this loud dripping sound for a couple of days and I've searched everywhere but I can't really locate where it's coming from.

Then all of a sudden yesterday, there appeared a large circle on the kitchen ceiling above the sink that has started dripping this brownish red gooey colored stuff and the spot has now gotten pretty big. I have two buckets under the leak on the floor by the sink. Could you come out and take a look?" "Yes, sure little lady, I can, but I can tell you right now, in an old house like that one... it being a two story house and being old, a leak could be coming from several places. It could be in the upstairs plumbing

96

or from the attic or the roof. It could be coming from a number of places so, I'll just have to take a look around." "I understand," said Kelly. "Well, he said will you be home tomorrow?" "I can be here, she said. What time will you be coming?" "I guess fairly early he replied. I can come over in the morning after I finish up here; how about around nine o'clock?" "Ok" replied Kelly. "That will be great. I will see you then."

The next morning Kelly watched through the curtains as Mr. Saunders got out of his truck. He looked in his late forties. He was tall with still a fairly good build. He had graying brown hair and walked with a slight limp. He stood in the front yard for a moment with one hand in his back pocket and looking up at the sky while finishing his cigarette. He suddenly spun around towards the street like someone had called his name. Then he dropped his cigarette on the sidewalk and crushed it with his shoe. As he started up the stairs to the front door Kelly quickly put her dogs in the sunroom and ran back to the front door to greet him. She waited for his knock. "Kelly?" he asked. "Yes sir," she said trying to cover the awkwardness of meeting this man she figured she already knew too much about from the Westbrook's. A man who might have been responsible for the death of Joe Hardy the previous owner and had possibly been his rival.

"Good morning she said, please come on in." She smiled and walked quickly in front of him, slightly turning her head and looking back over her shoulder as she escorted him to the kitchen while remarking how incredibly cold the weather was that morning. He agreed as she walked directly to the kitchen sink and pointed up at the now half dry red-brown circles on the ceiling. "I see," was his only remark about the stain. "What's above here?" he asked. Kelly replied, "One of the bedrooms. You're welcome to go up and look around if you want to. I was up there this morning and the floors looked dry." "Well, water could be coming in from a roof leak or wall leak, he said. Do you mind if I take a look?" "No sir. Like I said, please go right ahead and have a look for yourself. You're the expert, said Kelly.

The light switch is on the left, inside the doorway." He left to inspect the upstairs bedroom over the kitchen. She didn't go with him since she didn't want to be alone with him upstairs. Kelly could hear him walking to the closet and opening the door, then walking around in the bedroom and then walking down the hall.

He was back down stairs within a few minutes. "Well, he said, I didn't see any signs of a water leak. The fireplace looks dry and both bathrooms look ok. There could be a leak in the pipes, he added. You say you have been hearing dripping sounds?" "Yes sir," said Kelly, "you didn't hear anything?" "No," he replied, "I didn't hear any dripping but I'll tell you what I need to do, he said. I need to get my helper to come out here to check the roof for leaks." "Yes sir, she said, I thought the leak might be coming from the attic because I first heard the dripping sound when I was in the bedroom you were in, but when I got out in the hall it was much louder and it sounded like it was coming from the attic. I climbed up there but as soon as I got up there and started looking around the dripping stopped. From what I could see everything looked dry. There are a few boxes up there and they looked dry as well." "Yes mam," replied Mr. Saunders. "Well, he said, I'll have my helper take a look up there when he comes in. I'll get him out here tomorrow."

"Well ok," he said turning around and staring up at the circles on the ceiling again. "I wonder why the stain is red and brown Kelly asked." "I don't know," he answered. "I guess it could be some kind of stain mixing with the leak." He glanced down and then looked at Kelly and wiped the corners of this mouth with his hand and replied "Otherwise, do you like it here?" "I do," she said. "I'm just still trying to get settled in. Maybe after this leak is taken care of it will start feeling more like home, but I guess in an old house like this you will always have one problem or another."

He glanced around the room and said "yeah, in an old house you always do." Then he said, "I use to date the lady who lived here." "Really?" said Kelly pretending she didn't know about

Cindy. "Yep" he said, "We dated in high school. She was my first love and you never forget your first love." "Yep," he said again, "after school she left for college and we never, you know, got things going again." He continued on; "Sometimes things just don't work out." "Yes sir," said Kelly. "Sometimes they don't the way you want them to." Mr. Saunders continued, "She met Joe in Florida and they moved back to live here after her mother died." Kelly replied "Yes, Mr. Westbrook told me her husband, Joe fell off the roof and died while ya'll were putting on a new roof." "Yep" he replied. "That was a bad thing that happened. I was here helping put on the roof when he fell."

He looked up again at the circled ceiling and said "It was a terrible thing." "Yep, it was." "We finished putting the roof on for Cindy after the accident. Yeah, I believe it was about five years ago. Then she moved back to Florida. Anyways, I will have Steve drop by and look in the attic and on the roof tomorrow." Then he added "there could be just some loose shingles that may be causing the leak or a leaking pipe but we'll find it. Can he call you at work?" "Yes sir, replied Kelly. He can call me there anytime. Here is my card. I just want it repaired before it gets worse and I have a bigger problem to deal with."

CHAPTER 25

The next day was Tuesday. Kelly was not satisfied because she never got a chance to ask Mr. Saunders any questions about the relationship he had with Joe and she wanted to know how the roof accident happened. Later that morning at work she received a call from Mr. Saunders's helper Steve. He began, "Mr. Saunders said you might have a leak on your roof." "Yes sir" replied Kelly. "The leak is coming from the kitchen ceiling and it's a real mess. How soon can you come out?" she asked. "You live in the Hardy house right?" he asked. "Yes, that's right" replied Kelly. "Do you need the address?" "No" he replied. "I know where it is." "Let's see," he said, the earliest I can get there today is around 3:00 because I am working on another job but I should be through by then. Will that be ok?" "I guess that will be ok," said Kelly. "Alright" he replied, "I'll see you then." Kelly left work around 2:00 PM to be at home for Mr. Saunders's helper to arrive. When she heard a car door slam around 3:00 PM she peered out the front door window.

She watched as this young guy got out of his truck and walked towards the house tripping up the stairs on his way to the door. "Wow, he's really cute," she thought "but wait a minute. He looks just like the guy I saw downtown the other day. He's the guy that was watching me from across the street. I can't believe it. It's really him. I know it's him. Don't tell me he works for Mr. Saunders. Wow, small world. I wonder if he'll recognize me. I guess I'll soon find out." She suddenly felt very awkward.

He knocked on the door. Kelly took a deep breath. He impatiently hit the door again with three more quick knocks before she opened it. "Hi, are you Kelly?" "Yes I am," she replied. "I'm Steve" he said. "Hi Steve," she said cheerfully. "Come on in and I'll show you where the leak is." She looked at him and said, "Like I told you on the phone the leak is in the kitchen ceiling, it's this way." She noticed he kept looking down and wouldn't look directly at her. She headed towards the kitchen with him following behind. "He is so cute and I am so nervous," she thought. "I brought a ladder to check out the roof if I need to" he said. "Ok that's good" she replied. She thought, "I wonder if he recognizes me from the other day." Then he said "Old man Saunders said you think the leak might be coming from the attic."

"Well, said Kelly I told him I started hearing dripping sounds when I was in the upstairs bedroom. I checked that room and the dripping sounds weren't coming from that room. The ceiling looked dry. I checked the closet and the floor but I didn't hear the dripping sound or see anything wet but I could still hear the dripping so I walked out into the hall and the sounds seemed louder out there. I didn't see a leak on the ceiling and nothing was wet out there. So, I thought the sounds must be coming from the attic. I went up in the attic and thought I had discovered the leak because I could have sworn I heard the dripping when I got up there but the dripping sound only lasted for a second and then suddenly stopped. I looked around a little bit and everything looked dry. All I know, she said is that there is that huge spot on the kitchen ceiling, as you can see, that is dripping down in the sink and is getting larger."

When they reached the kitchen Kelly turned around to face him and pointed up to the ceiling. He looked up and said. "Oh yeah, I see." "Yeah" he said, "that leak might be coming from the inside pipes in the kitchen." When their eyes finally met he glanced up and down her body. He smiled and she smiled back at him. "You need to look up there" Kelly said smiling and pointing at the red brown circle on the ceiling that had suddenly become moist again while it had appeared dry that morning. Steve glanced up. "Wow" he said, "it looks like it's getting larger and it's turned red." "How long has it been like that?" he asked. Kelly replied, "I guess about a week now. It has been a brownish red color but today it is really red." "Did Saunders look upstairs?" "Yes, she said, he checked the bedroom that's right above the leak and he said he checked both bathrooms too and said he couldn't see any signs of a leak. Like I told him, I looked in the attic and I heard dripping but it stopped. He didn't go up there but said you would check the attic for me. He said you would bring some roof sealer with you." Steve just smiled. He seemed to suddenly zone out and became totally fixed on Kelly. While she talked on about hearing the dripping sound she could see his eyes wandering up and down her body again.

He had this half crocked smile on his face and although she continued talking about the leak, she was becoming distracted each time she glanced at his piercing blue eyes that were watching every move she made. "Well, she said hoping to break his spell for a moment. The attic is a little too spooky for me, so be my guest and see if you think the leak is coming from up there." He felt around in his jacket pockets and said "let me go to my truck and get a flash light." "Oh I have one that might do, said Kelly. Let me get it for you." She opened the kitchen drawer and retrieved her big flashlight. Steve was making her nervous watching every move she made. When she handed the flashlight to him he smiled at her again and she reciprocated and smiled at him. He then walked to the sink and looked up at the circle again. He got a chair from the table and said "Is this chair pretty sturdy?"

Before she could answer he was standing in it and pushing on the ceiling with the end of the flashlight. Although the circle was not dripping the red brown goo it still appeared to have gotten larger. He stared at it for a moment like he was in a trance then suddenly began blinking his eyes. He got down from the chair and for some reason he leaned over the sink to the window. It looked like he was straining to see the yard below. He then stood back and looked up at the ceiling again. Kelly thought that was kind of strange but she figured he must be determining where the leak could be coming from.

"Well, he said after a moment, I'll go up and check out the bedroom and the bathrooms and then look in the attic." Kelly could hear him walking around above her head. It sounded exactly

like the other times she had heard footsteps there and that confirmed to her that she really had heard footsteps upstairs. He seemed to be gone for at least ten minutes or more. She finally went to the bottom of the staircase and called out. "Steve, did you find anything?" He came down in a few minutes. "Well, I saw a couple of places near the wall in the attic that were damp and I think rain may have gotten in at the window and ran down inside the wall. I pushed the window down more securely. That might have fixed part of the problem."

Kelly asked "You said you brought a ladder. Are you not going to check up on the roof?" Steve replied "I would but it's started raining again and the roof may be slippery right now. Let's just see if closing the window helped first." "Hum ok, said Kelly, I don't recall the window being open when I was up there." "Well, it was a little, said Steve and it's been raining a lot lately. You may want be careful walking around up there. There's some loose wiring hanging out of the walls. If any of it is exposed wiring, and it is wet you could get shocked and it could even be a fire hazard." "That sounds dangerous" said Kelly. "I guess I will have to have an electrician check it out." "I can check it out for you he said but right now it's almost dark up there. I can come back and check out the wiring for you during a week day." "Well, ok" she replied.

"Well, he said grinning how do you like living here so far?" "Oh, I love this house," she said. "If I could just get this leak taken care of I could enjoy it more, but I guess there's always got to be something to worry about" she said with a laugh. She thought to herself, "If he only knew what it has been like for me since I moved in here." She needed desperately to talk to someone. "You don't think you'll get lonely living in this big place by yourself?" he asked. "Wow, she thought it's amazing how you can know someone for ten minutes and they start getting personal."

"Anyway, why is he so sure I live here by myself?" She said, "This house is big." He kept smiling at her while his eyes sparkled with mischief. She had to admit he had gotten her attention. His rugged handsome face and those beautiful blue eyes were like blue lights dancing all over her, turning her inside out. With his mouth fixed in that crooked smile he watched her as she talked to him while leaning against the sink. She tried to engage in small talk about the house but was beginning to feel a little bit uncomfortable as he began inching closer to her. It seemed he wanted to socialize more than work.

Suddenly, he reached out and lightly stroked the upper part of her arm with his fingers. She smiled but gently pulled back trying to stay composed by taking both of her arms and folding them in front of her. He kept smiling while talking and then leaned over towards her and with his hand smoothed her hair back exposing her ear. Kelly playfully pushed him back from her but he surprised her by leaning forward and trying to kiss her ear. She glanced at the clock on the wall. It was five o'clock. She tried to think of a way to end his playful parlor games because he seemed to be getting a little too aggressive for her. "Are you thirsty she asked? I have tea, coke, water." He glanced at the clock. "Oh it's 5:00 o'clock, quit'n time," he replied. Have you got a beer?" "I think so" Kelly replied.

"That might not have been the right question to have asked him" she thought. She didn't really want him to stay any longer and decided that after drinking this one beer she would tell him she had somewhere to go. As she walked to the refrigerator she could feel his eyes were glued on her and he kept clearing his throat until she reached the refrigerator. She returned and smiling at him, handed him a beer. He pulled the top off the can and took a big drink, burped and leaned back against the kitchen cabinet. The heat had warmed the house and after only half a beer Kelly became more at ease with him but still felt a little nervous.

He kept watching her while she talked. Then all of a sudden he put his beer down and walked over to her. He took her face in his hands and while looking in her eyes kissed her gently, holding the kiss for a long moment like he was attaching his lips to hers. She was left mesmerized when he finally let go. He pulled her to him again and began kissing her lips softly prying her mouth open with his mouth to insert his tongue. Her body had become relaxed from the beer and became more responsive as he pressed himself against her. Her insides felt like putty. She couldn't move. She was wrapped in a state of perpetual bliss and aching for more. She opened her eyes. Her head was swimming at this point.

He leaned forward and kissed her again. She closed her eyes sinking deeper into the eternal bliss he was giving her. But then he was suddenly holding her closer to him and pressing himself hard up against her to where she could hardly move. She tried to push him back with her arms that were positioned up against his chest but he restrained her by quickly grabbing both arms and forcing them behind her back to where she couldn't move. She yelled out in pain and began struggling to get free. About that time the door bell rang. Kelly was startled but relieved. Steve released her and said in a discouraged voice "who could that be?" They both went to the front door. Kelly peered out the window. "It's Mr. Saunders" she told Steve. "Oh that's just great" he said. Kelly opened the door and said "hello." Mr. Saunders looked past Kelly when he saw Steve standing in the living room. "Hey Steve" he said. "Steve you left the roof sealer in the front office. I was driving by and thought you might need it."

"Yeah, thanks" said Steve. "I guess I forgot to put it in the truck. I might need it tomorrow." "Did you find anything in the attic?" Mr. Saunders asked. Steve replied, "The only leak I found was at one of the windows in the attic. The back window was open a little. I closed it real tight so if there was a leak coming from there I sealed it off by closing that window. I don't think I'll need the sealant right now since it's raining. There's also some loose wiring up in the attic that I'm going to take care of when I have more daylight. I didn't see a leak from inside the house. The only leak I can see is in the kitchen ceiling and it's not dripping right now. I think I might need to get into the ceiling and try to find out where it's coming from. Also, since it's raining I can't check the roof today."

He looked at Kelly and said "If I do go into the kitchen ceiling I will need to turn off the water to fix it." Kelly replied, "Ok, whatever you need to do." Mr. Saunders turned and opened the front door and walked out on the porch. "Well, I'm gone, he said. You take care of this little lady and I'll see you in the morning Steve." "All right," said Steve. Kelly shut the front door. "Thanks, old man Saunders, said Steve. That was perfect timing."

After Mr. Saunders left Kelly felt very uncomfortable with Steve. They stood in the living room just staring at each other. Kelly said, "Steve I think you'd better go." Steve said, "I'm sorry, I just got carried away. It won't happen again." She took a deep breath and said "thanks for coming out and looking for the leak. I just wish it could have been fixed." Steve told her that the best way to fix the leak may be to go into the ceiling and check for busted pipes or rotten wood and if he can find the leak, he would then patch the ceiling and paint it for her. He said, "then it will be good as new and you'll have no more problems." He said he would check with her the next week about coming out. She agreed but they didn't set a date and at that point she just wanted him out of the house. He then said "call me if you need me." He grabbed his tool chest, and headed for the door.

After Steve left, Kelly wandered through the house for the rest of the evening walking around and thinking about all the events that had occurred that day. She was trying to make sense of everything that was going on in her life. How far would things have gone with Steve if Mr. Saunders had not interrupted them? She knew she might have had no control over what would have happened next. And she knew if she had rejected Steve, things could have gotten out of hand. Was she discovering that maybe she wasn't as secure as she thought she was?

She had been through a lot of changes since her parents had passed and had been living alone for awhile in that house and was having a hard time coping with all that had happened to her since she moved in. Her life as it was up to that very day may have been affecting her in ways she hadn't realized. Maybe she was just human and needed someone to be close to. "I do need someone to be close to" she thought, but not that way. She had to admit her experience with Steve was a definite wakeup call that got her thinking that she was almost forced to have sex with a complete stranger. She suddenly began to change her mind about Steve.

CHAPTER 26

Kelly tried to keep a positive attitude the following week. The circle on the ceiling looked like it was drying up so she was back to making more decisions about decorating the house until one afternoon a week later, right after work, she was in the kitchen feeding her dogs when she heard voices like she had before except they were arguing and footsteps walking loudly back and forth above her head. The voices were muffled so she couldn't understand what they were saying. She thought at first the voices were coming from outside. She looked out both kitchen windows but saw no one. She listened again. The talking suddenly stopped. She then heard loud footsteps above her head again. The sounds seemed to echo throughout the house. She then heard the sounds of feet shuffling like in a fight. Afterwards there was a thud sound like someone had fallen upstairs right above her head. She stood as still as possible looking up at the ceiling and listening. She could feel her heart pounding rapidly in her chest.

Her temples pulsated in her head. She was terrified, and completely frozen in fear. Suddenly, she felt a great force of icy cold wind rush passed her making a swishing sound. It was so strong the glasses and china in the wall cabinet clanged against the cabinet glass doors and the cabinets shook. Then the back door trembled and creaked like it was going to crack open from pressure. Then suddenly all was quiet again. Kelly remained in a frozen trance unable to move. Her eyes searched all around the room as she waited for the next dreaded occurrence. Her only thought was to escape and to get out of the house. If she could only reach the back door she would be free and would never look back. She tried to step to the right but she couldn't move. She tried to extend her right arm but couldn't. Her limbs ached and her stomach churned.

Suddenly she heard loud dripping. At first it was drip, drip, with least a second in between each drip. Then the dripping sounds began to run together and became a loud trickle sound. The sound echoed throughout the house. All of a sudden Kelly felt released from the powers that had paralyzed her and she caught her breath. She was able to move her body by falling forward on the sink. As she grasped the edge of the sink she could see something on the ceiling from the corner of her eye. What had been the dried brown circled stains for over a week had now become blood red again. The bright red substance was forming a large red circle and began to drip into the sink and on the floor. She pushed a dish towel under the dripping and stepped back from the sink. She stood in front of the sink watching in horror and disbelief as the blood colored liquid dripped down into the sink and made its way slowly down the drain.

She cupped her hands over her mouth and stepped back. As she did she saw a body fall passed the kitchen window hitting the ground with a loud thud. She gasped as tears welled in her eyes. She began repeating to herself "I am getting out of here and I will never come back." She realized she was again paralyzed with fear and could hardly move. She knew a body was on the ground beside the house and she had to go and see for herself. It was getting dusky dark. In slow motion she reached for the flashlight in the drawer. "I have got to see if a body really fell passed this window" she thought. She reached for the back door and opened it. She felt a sense of relief because all seemed so normal as she looked across the back yard. She could hear people talking across the alley, a dog was barking in the distance.

Her dogs came running up to the back door. They had been outside all afternoon. She had completely forgotten to let them in. She knew that if they had heard or seen a body fall they would have started barking immediately. She put them inside and walked down the back steps. Her head was now hurting from a pounding headache and her heart was beating fast. She turned the flashlight on. Her stomach churned and her hands were shaking. She walked slowly around to the side of the house. With her eyes starring wide open she took a quick look expecting to see more horror but there was no body lying on the ground. She glanced up to the top of the house. All the windows were shut.

The darkness began to surround her and the cold air seemed to invade her entire mind and body. She ran back inside the house and locked the door. She looked around in the kitchen. The dripping had stopped and as she listened all seemed to be quiet again. She ran throughout the house frantically opening every door and closet. She had to make sure she was alone in the house. She searched every room including the basement but didn't have the nerve to go into the attic. She had to finally conclude that something else was going on here, something more like a haunting. Kelly pondered then made a startling realization.

"If this is a haunting, then the ceiling is not really leaking but a leak for some reason forms and makes itself known at certain times by some entity." "The blood circle on the ceiling must be a sign, a message, which materializes from the entity that is haunting this house." But regardless, after she saw the body fall and there was not a real body there, she was finally convinced that there was no real leak in the ceiling after all and that the circles that were forming and dripping from the ceiling and the dripping sounds were from a spirit trying to reveal its presence. She didn't want to admit it to herself but she was now becoming convinced that there was something else going on here that involved the attic and the death of Joseph Hardy.

CHAPTER 27

It was going on 10:00 PM. The house was quiet again. Kelly lay down on the couch and in her state of desperation decided to turn to the only source that could really calm her down and give her inner peace. She was emotionally drained. She relaxed and began to concentrate and to meditate. She was walking down a long hallway. The walls were white. At the end of the hall to the right was an entrance leading to a dark corridor. She didn't look to the right. She knew there was nothing there but a long tunnel of total darkness. But to her immediate left was an old wooden door with a small window at the top. Light streamed in through the small window that beckoned her. She opened the door and stepped out into a garden with the stone floor. She was always bare footed in this meditation. The sun was shining and the stones were beginning to warm from the sun. It was going on mid-morning.

There were two other doors in the garden; the one door to her right and the one straight ahead of her. She sensed that people were around but didn't see anyone. She turned and walked to her left down the stone walkway. At the end of the walkway to the right was the entrance to an outside temple of prayer. She was going back to this place of prayer that she always went to when she was in need of spiritual guidance. She entered the garden temple area. There were a few old cement benches with tables in the mist of it. The entire area had a tall white wall that surrounded it and was covered in vines. There was the large white chiseled out piece of stone. Kelly knelt there and prayed. Her prayers always started with please forgive me for my sins and fill me with your holy spirit. She soon drifted off to sleep. The next thing she remembered was waking up feeling ice cold and standing in the middle of the back yard. She realized she must have been sleep walking which she knew she had never done before. In a frozen daze she ran quickly into the house and upstairs to her bedroom. She had a severe migraine and felt very exhausted. She put her warmest socks on and threw on her long robe. She glanced at the clock. It was a little past three. She wondered how long she had been outside. She sat on the edge of her bed. Suddenly she remembered. It was now coming back to her. After meditating she fell asleep. She had a dream about Joe Hardy.

She dreamed she and some other people were fixing up the house. She saw Joe Hardy talking with a man. As she peered down this long dark hall, she could see him and this man standing together at the far end of the hall. She could also see them standing together and talking somewhere outside in the day light. She could see part of Joe's face. Although his face looked blurred she knew it was him. The next thing she remembered about the dream was Joe was reaching for her hand. She reached out to him but he disappeared. She remembered that someone told her in her dream he had fallen off the roof. Kelly knew that during her dream she must have willed herself in her sleep outside to search for Joe on the roof and for answers to what had happened to him. She then realized he had tried to communicate with her in her dreams before she ever saw the house. He was the man in her dream that was trying to give her a key. He knew if Kelly had the key to open the door to the house, that she would be able to reveal the truth about his death.

It's not really that complicated she thought. He died from falling off the roof and now he is haunting this house, but why? That was the real question. It was hard to imagine or understand any of what was happening. It all seemed really crazy to Kelly and too farfetched from anything she spiritually believed in. Kelly was realizing more and more that if this is a haunting by the man who fell off the roof and died here, then he has an agenda. He has a purpose in doing what he is doing and he is trying to tell Kelly something. Kelly pondered more about the reasons that she was hearing the dripping sounds, seeing the blood drip from the ceiling and hearing voices and scuffling and then seeing a body fall passed the window.

She was becoming convinced that the unexplained events that were going on was because Joe was in his way trying to relay to her what had happened to him. Kelly concluded that since she was continuously hearing more than one voice and more than one set of footsteps, that maybe Joe's death wasn't an accident. He may have fallen off the roof or he may have been murdered on the roof, or even somewhere in the house and then pushed off the roof. She wanted to pick Steve's brain about Mr. Saunders. After all, he worked for him and if anyone would know the real relationship that existed between him and Joe, Steve should know.

Kelly went through the rest of the night without any more disturbances but felt tired and worn out the next morning from the lack of sleep. As she entered the kitchen she glanced up at the ceiling. "The monster has gone back in its cave" she thought. The ceiling appeared still damp with the brownish red stains but not dripping. "At times everything here is quiet and peaceful and seems almost normal again" she thought. She desperately wanted things to be back like they were when she first moved in. She wondered if she would ever be able to enjoy the beautiful home that she remembered buying. She glanced over her shoulder to check her phone messages before grabbing her keys and heading out the back door. It was a relief to know that outside the back door there would be some sense of reality as she headed for work.

She anticipated a busy week ahead as usual beginning with the company's monthly bills that had to be written out and mailed to the accountant. It had now been a week since the last house activity and her sleep walking episode. Kelly knew things had gotten to the point that she needed to talk to someone about what she had been experiencing. She reached for Steve's business card that read Saunders Roofing Co. She didn't want to contact Steve about fixing the roof after what had happened between them but Kelly had never had a chance to ask him any questions about Bill Saunders and after talking to Faye she had suspected that he might have had something to do with Joe's death. And even though the ceiling had not been fixed and at this point she concluded it may never be fixed until the mystery around Joe's death was solved, she still wanted to pursue all avenues to get the ceiling leak repaired.

After all, Steve had promised that he would come back out to fix the attic wiring and tear out the kitchen ceiling but she hadn't heard a word from him. The ceiling was still leaking and had not been repaired by the company that put on the roof and claimed they would make all repairs good as in their contract five years prior. Kelly had become agitated with Bill Saunders and Steve for not coming back to repair her ceiling by now. But regardless she still wanted to talk to Steve about Mr. Saunders and maybe he could tell her more about the relationship that Joe and Bill had and more details about the so-called accident. She was now convinced that Joe was trying to communicate with her about his death and she needed to get more answers so, somehow she had to get to the bottom of what had really happened to him.

CHAPTER 28

That morning at work, she picked up the phone and called the number on the Saunders's Roofing business card that Steve had given her. Steve answered the phone "Saunders Roofing." "Hello" said Kelly. "Is this Steve?" "Yes, it is" he replied. "Hey Steve, this is Kelly Brown. How have you been?" "Oh, pretty fair he replied. What's up Kelly?" he asked. "Well, the kitchen ceiling is still leaking Steve" replied Kelly. "I was wondering if you would mind coming by sometime tomorrow to take another look at this mess again." "I was going to call you about that" replied Steve. "Now that the rain seems to have stopped for awhile, I wanted to look up in the attic again and on the roof. I don't usually work on Saturdays, but I could come by around 1:00 tomorrow if that's ok." "Ok," she said. "After you check for the leak would you like some lunch? I plan on grilling some steaks! You've got to eat lunch. How does that sound?" "Well, I don't want you to go to any trouble for me," he replied. "Oh, it won't be any trouble" said Kelly. "They'll practically grill themselves and I would like to have your company if you can behave yourself, and there's also something I wanted to ask you about." "Oh, ok," he said. "I'll see you around 1:00."

Steve arrived Saturday a little passed 2:00 PM and knocked lightly on the front door. Kelly opened the door and said "Hi, you're late." He smiled as he walked passed her carrying his tool box then turned around and tried to give her a hug with his free arm but she shied away. He then followed her to the kitchen.

Placing her hands on her hips she stopped at the kitchen sink and looked up at the leak and said, "That spot was leaking reddish brownish gooey looking stuff just a couple of days ago and now it gone. I don't understand it. It gets wet all of a sudden and gets bigger and bigger. Then it starts dripping this brown reddish stuff that looks like blood and then all of a sudden it stops dripping and gradually dries up leaving that big ugly stain."

Kelly continued, "If you could only experience it day by day and see what I've been going through. It's like it's alive and when it's hungry it gets red and drips bloody brown goo and then it gradually stops and looks almost dry again. Even the color of it fades from red to brown. You have got to find out where it's coming from. Why do you think it's that color?" she asked. Steve eyes were fixed on the spot. "I don't know Kelly, he replied unless it's from the wood stain that's on the floor of the upstairs bedroom being mixed with water leaking down." "I'll check the bedroom out again he said.

Maybe Saunders missed something when he was up there looking around. Maybe the leak is coming from in the fireplace or chimney. I'll go on up now and have another look." He turned and left for the living room. "Ok, Kelly said loudly as he reached the staircase. I'll be on the carport getting the grill ready." She stacked the charcoal on the grill on the carport and had the steaks ready to put on. She set the kitchen table for dinner and opened a bottle of wine. She could hear Steve walking around in the bedroom above her. After a while she heard the stairs being pulled down to the attic. He finally returned after about 15 minutes.

"See anything? What's the verdict?" she asked. "Well, he replied, if the leak is coming from the bedroom floor I can't tell from the surface. The floor is dry and the attic floor appears dry too. The flooring would have to be pulled up. I couldn't see where any water had leaked in where I had closed the window in the attic. I can check the roof but I don't see any place on the ceiling that is wet in the attic and the floor is dry too. I actually have a better idea. I mentioned this to you before. I think what I need to do is tear out the wet spot on the ceiling in the kitchen. It's probably a leak from a busted pipe." "Ok" Kelly replied. "How soon can you do that?" "I can do it now or later," he said. "The only thing is the water will need to be cut off and you're using it right now to cook.

I could go ahead and start on it after we eat. But if I open the ceiling up and it's leaking, like I said, I will have to cut the water off and I have no way of knowing how big of a job it will be. I would really like to start working on it early one morning maybe after you leave for work." "Ok, next week would be good she said, the sooner the better." "Ok," said Steve. "Let me check with old man Saunders and see what else he has lined up and I will give you a call." She then asked Steve if he was hungry. He smiled and said "oh, I guess a little." He then pulled out a pack of cigarettes from his shirt pocket and lit one. She had the charcoal starter in her hand as she turned to go out of the back door. "I'm going to light the charcoals she said. I'll be right back." "Ok baby" he replied."

When she returned she sat down beside him at the kitchen table and watched him finish his cigarette. All of a sudden she found herself saying things she hadn't planned on saying to him. "You know when we met, she began, I thought you looked familiar." "Really?" he said cocking his head inquisitively to the side. She gave him a serious look and said "You don't remember ever seeing me before?" "You know before the first time you came here to look at the leak?" He just starred at her with furrowed brows. "No," "I don't think so" he said. She continued, "I'm pretty sure it was you. I was downtown headed to my office one morning and I had stopped to buy a paper. You were standing on the corner across the street in front of my office in the Brown Building. We looked at each other. I remember you were smoking a cigarette and you looked at me and I smiled. I think you smiled too. Then you flipped your cigarette out into the street. "Well, I'm sorry, I swear I don't remember, he said."

She laughed and added "Well, there's no reason you should remember I guess, but I remember you." "Oh I don't know," he replied, grinning while squeezing and rubbing her arm. "I think I would definitely remember if I had ever seen you before." Kelly laughed and remarked, "Well, if it wasn't you, you have an identical twin." She added, "I recognized you the moment I saw you at the front door when you first came to look at the ceiling. I just thought it was strange I guess because I wondered who you were the first time I saw you and then I actually got to meet you. I thought, "Wow! Small World." "Were you glad to see me again?" he asked. "Well, she grinned and replied, "Like I said, I did wonder who you were when I saw you that day."

She smiled at him again and excused herself to go put the steaks on the grill. When she returned she poured them each a glass of wine and returned to her chair and said "Steve, I've really needed to talk to someone about the strange things that have been happening to me since I moved in here." "Strange things?" Steve asked. "Yes, some real strange things have been going on here" she replied. "Stranger than blood dripping from the ceiling?" he asked. Then he stood up to do his imitation of the mummy with his arms out stretched, his eyes opened wide and his fingers wiggling as he walked stiff legged towards Kelly and said "I'm coming for you Kelly you cannot escape me." Kelly squirmed, "Seriously" she said, "it all started when I moved in here or actually before I moved in here.

When I tell you about this please try not to be too judgmental because I am not lying ok?" Steve nodded so she proceeded. "It really all began when I had a dream about this house and then I found myself looking at this house and then wanting to buy it. The first day I looked at it I saw this man in the back yard and from time to time I still see this same man in the back yard. I have seen him four times now. That's not counting the dreams I have about him. The first time I thought he was just someone looking at the house or maybe someone Mr. Westbrook had working on the house. But that was before I bought it and moved in. Since then like I said I keep seeing him and dreaming about him. What is so weird is that he has the same clothes on every time I see him. He's always standing in the back yard looking up at the attic window and like I said he's always dressed the same.

Then there was another man hanging around in the alley one night when I took out the trash. It was pretty late, I think about 10:30 PM. This man was standing out under a tree in the alley smoking a cigarette. He was just standing there in freezing 30 degree weather just quietly watching me. He never said a word. I dropped the trash and ran back to the house. I think he was behind me. It scared me to death." "Well, it wasn't me," replied Steve, "I'm not a stalker." "I know you're not," said Kelly. "I'm not implying it was you. But actually, this guy was about your size and height. But so is the man I keep seeing in the back yard. I keep having these dreams about this man and this house. Like I said he's always standing in the yard in the same spot under the myrtle tree close to the house and always has this sad look on his face. There have been some other really strange things that have happened. But I know if I tell you, you'll think I'm losing my mind.

Let me get the steaks before they burn and we'll eat." She returned with the steaks, refilled their wine glasses and they began to eat. After Steve had eaten a couple of bites he asked, "So what other things have been going on?" "First let me ask you something she said, did you know Joe Hardy?" "No, I didn't really know him that well," he replied. "He worked with me and old man Saunders on a couple of jobs." "What did he look like?" she asked. "Why?" asked Steve. "Well, maybe I found a picture. I'm just curious," said Kelly. Steve replied "Uh, he was I guess, he had brown hair." "Was it light or dark?" she asked. "I guess medium brown" he said. She asked, "What color were his eyes? Was he tall, short?" "He was I guess six feet and about 170 or 180. I don't know about his eyes" he said. "How old?" she asked. He remarked, "Maybe 40 or so." "Ok, that helps," she said.

"Did you find some pictures?" he asked. "No," she answered, I wish I could find a picture." "I told you I have seen this man in the back yard a couple of times since I have been in here. Anyway, this one time that I saw this guy in the yard, I tried to talk to him. It was pouring down rain and he was just standing there. I opened the back door and in one split second he was gone. I ran around the house and he had just disappeared." Steve rolled his eyes and replied, "Well who ever this guy is he's got to be hanging around for some reason. He may be planning on breaking in. You need to report him to the police. They can at least be on the lookout for him. What does he look like?" he questioned. "He fits the description you just gave me of Joe Hardy." "Well, he can't be Joe Hardy, said Steve because Joe Hardy is dead. He was the owner of this house and he fell off the roof."

Kelly looked at Steve and replied, "I know he was the previous owner and that he is deceased. But let me tell you this man is real spooky looking. His skin is real strange and ashy colored. He always has on a blue jean shirt, dark blue jeans and those orangey brown colored lace up work boots and he's always just standing in the yard starring up at the roof." Steve stared out in space for a couple of seconds and then replied, "Like I said you should report this guy to the police and they can be on the lookout for him. He sounds like a bone-a-fide nut. He's probably the same man that you saw in the alley. I would report what has been going on" said Steve. Kelly retrieved the rest of the wine and sat back down beside Steve.

"That's not all she continued, since I have been here, lights in the house come on at night after I have turned them off. I go to bed and turn the upstairs hall light off and I get up the next morning and the light is on. A vase on the mantel fell on the hearth and broke the day I bought it when I know it was secure on the mantel. One night, in the middle of the night I woke up and heard a loud crash downstairs. Do you see those hanging pots on the pot rack?" She pointed her finger towards the rack." Steve replied, "Yeah?" "Well," she said, "the rack was swinging back and forth and all the pots were in the floor. The rack was still attached to the ceiling and when I entered the kitchen the rack slowly came to a stop. The kitchen cabinets and the dishes shake all the time like in an earthquake tremor." Steve bowed his head down and then slung his head back combing his fingers through his hair. He took a deep breath and said "do you really expect me to believe all this?" "I know! It sounds surreal," she said. "It is surreal to me! You know these things have really happened to me in this house. They still do happen. No one has been in here with me to see this stuff happen but me. The worst part is that leak above the sink that looks like blood. Sometimes it drips down and other times it almost clears up and disappears like it is now. I know when it is going to start dripping because I will hear footsteps and voices arguing and scuffling coming from upstairs in the attic. And you're not ready for what happened last week." Steve interrupted her.

"How can you live here if all this is really happening?" "I'm scared," she said, but I want to find out why this is going on. If it keeps getting worse I know I will have to move out and sell the place. Maybe you can tell me, on the day that Joe Hardy fell from the roof, do you know what happened?" "What happened?" Steve replied. Yes, she said "I really want to know exactly how he died. Did Mr. Saunders tell you?"

Then she added, "Right after I bought this house I was talking to Mr. Westbrook about the previous owners and he said that Mr. Saunders had helped Joe Hardy put on the roof and that Bill really liked Joe a lot. Which I can't figure out because I know from Faye, Mr. Westbrook's daughter that Bill had or might even still have a fatal attraction for Cindy Joe's wife." Steve laughed and threw back his head again and said, "Saunders liked him?" Hardy wanted to buy old man Saunders's business right out from under him. He had offered him a lot of money and Saunders had told him he would think about it. "Yeah, and he use to date Hardy's wife in high school. He had a bad fatal-attraction, mad crush on her. It got really messy.

I know her parents filed a restraining order to keep him away from her. Then they had to throw him in jail for ignoring the order. He use to follow her around everywhere she went. He was insanely jealous. She had to move to another state because of him. When she moved back here to take care of her mother before she died of cancer, the old man started coming around again. Then, out of the blue Hardy shows up. Cindy met him when she moved to Florida. They got married and moved back into the house. Boy, that really messed up old man Saunders plans. He might have pretended he liked him but I think he wanted her back husband or no husband. After Hardy died he started coming around again.

He took her out a couple of times trying to get back in her good graces but she moved back to Florida to live with some relatives." "So maybe his little plan of trying to get back with her didn't work?" said Kelly."Do you think he could have caused Joe's death?" "Well," said Steve "I really wouldn't put it past him to have lost it and done something crazy when he found out Cindy had a new man. Put it this way, Hardy's death was no loss to old man Saunders. It just gave him a better chance to get back with Cindy." "Wow" said Kelly. "You never can tell about people. When I talked to Mr. Saunders he sounded like he was sorry about what happened to Joe. He acted like he really liked him. "No, I don't think so" said Steve.

Kelly concluded that maybe Saunders might have been under suspicion so when Joe Hardy's name is brought up or the accident is mentioned he always talks up Joe Hardy so not to cast any suspicion on himself. Especially since everyone knew how crazy he had been about Cindy. "So, Kelly asked, "You say he was on the roof with him?" Steve stood up and took a deep breath and replied "Yep, somehow he fell or got pushed." "Wow", she said again. "Was there ever an investigation she asked?" "He died of a broken neck" replied Steve. "That's how they saw it. Which way is your bathroom he ask?" After he returned Steve didn't seem as interested in laying it on hot and heavy that evening as he did the first time they met. I guess the subject matter put a damper on things. He said he thought the steak may have settled the wrong way. He said he would call Kelly the first of the week about coming out one morning to tear out the bad place in the kitchen ceiling. Kelly agreed and after a couple more minutes of chit chat she walked Steve to the door. He stood at the door with his head down and his brows furrowed like he was in deep thought or worried about something. "Are you ok" she asked? "Yeah," I'm fine, he said. "It's my stomach." He gave her a quick hug, and said "You worn me out with all your wild tales." He then made a kind effort and said "If anything else crazy happens or you need to talk, call me I'll come right over, ok?" "Ok," thanks," she said. "Well, good night." "Good night" he said.

CHAPTER 29

Kelly couldn't get the idea out of her head that Bill Saunders might have actually killed Joe Hardy out of jealousy for Joe's wife Cindy, Bill's once sweetheart. That would explain, she guessed, why Joe, if it was Joe was haunting this house so that the truth about his death would be revealed to Kelly. If this was really true, there was only one thing left to do and that was to somehow prove it. Was Joe actually murdered and cannot rest? If so, if Bill Saunders didn't kill him then who did kill him? Kelly was confused and asked herself; "What is going on?" "I know I won't be able to take much more of this she thought before I will move out of this house."

She had never believed in ghosts, or hauntings or spirits or whatever, and had never had an experience before or given the subject more that a second thought. And now, she was actually witnessing first hand a number of strange events that she couldn't rationalize or explain to herself or explain to anyone else without looking like some kind of self-proclaimed psychic, ghost buster, witch, mental basket case and definitely the kind of nut-so job you would want to stay away from. "That was probably why Steve, the sex maniac went cold turkey on me and got out of here tonight" she thought. "He thinks I'm crazy. I shouldn't have said anything to him. Who wants to be around a crazy person? If he only knew about my psychic premonitions and dreams he would have really gotten a stomach ache." She knew as always some things are better left unsaid.

The days that followed were very busy at the office. Interest rates were down and people were buying houses again. It had been two weeks since she had last seen Steve. He had not called her about repairing the kitchen ceiling like he had promised he would. But she knew he wouldn't. He had never kept one promise that he had made. She decided that it was ok if he had been scared away because the more she thought about him the more frustrated she became. Needless to say he was actually a very strange person himself. After all, he had tried to force himself on her the first time they met although thankfully they were interrupted.

She had been in a situation with him where she was about to be forced to have sex with him and she had no means of self defense and no means of escaping from him. Was it such a mistake on her part for her to think it could be possible to meet some really good looking guy who she might have a normal relationship with? She wondered if he came on to all women that forcefully or just the ones like her that he knew he could have his way with. She wondered how many other women he had forced sex on. All she knew was she didn't want be get involved with someone who thought they could dominate her sexually and not show her an ounce of respect. Yes, she had been attracted to him because he was super fine looking but then she learned firsthand that looks can be deceiving. Kelly had wanted to like Steve. She wanted him to be a warm, gentle and caring person and at the same time strong and fearless. He was definitely not a romantic knight in shining armor. If there is such a man and if in reality she would really want such a man. She couldn't help but want to believe that inside of Steve there was a hero, just waiting for the right opportunity to show his true colors.

She needed someone she could trust and depend on. Someone who would stand by her and protect her at all costs and someone she could stand by and protect at all cost. She wanted to believe for his sake that somewhere inside of him there was a good caring person but then she had to face reality. It seems when people try to change each other that's when you can get into trouble. Kelly was a dreamer wanting to hold on to believing that this man that she had been attracted to was a better person inside than he even knew he was just because suddenly she couldn't get him out of her head. But you take a person that cannot change and does not ever reveal a good true side to you, you must not get caught on a Ferris wheel of endless hope that just keeps repeating itself over and over going nowhere and only puts you on an endless journey where you end up looking into the face of despair until finally you grow so weary you can't help yourself or find yourself anymore and then you become weak and you wonder how you got that way and you just long to have your old self back the way you were.

Kelly thought back about her future dream plan when she was younger. She dreamed of finishing college, getting married to her soul mate, having kids, a dog, a cat, a beautiful home and a fenced in back yard. She had met a lot of guys since then but she hadn't as of yet met her soul mate. She was not going to let her dreams get shattered. Steve had gotten her attention but she knew she had to put her fantasies about him in their place. She had to face it; he was not exactly husband or father material and not what she was looking for in a soul mate. She was actually shocked at how he had conducted himself in such an unprofessional manner while at her house. And now he hadn't kept his word about coming back to fix the ceiling. She was very upset and even considering calling a different roofing company to come out and look at the situation.

CHAPTER 30

Friday had rolled around again and sales had been good. Kelly and Kim had planned on having a drink together to unwind a little after work but it had turned out to be a longer day than they had anticipated and they ended up staying until after 6:00 PM so, they decided to do it another night. Instead, Kelly decided to go by the grocery store on the way home but her car hesitated to start in the parking lot. When she did get it started she drove straight home. The next morning she called her mechanic Charlie Benson at home. He had an auto repair shop and specialized in foreign car repairs. He came and picked her up, and took her to work. He called her later that morning and said he thought she had a bad starter switch and he would have to find one. He didn't have her car ready by the end of the day so Kim took her home.

Although the next day was Saturday and Kelly was at home without a car, Charlie said he would go to the shop and work on it and get her car to her by Saturday afternoon. Saturday morning around 10:00 AM the phone rang. Kelly was standing in the back yard with her dogs. By the time she reached the kitchen her voice mail had picked up. When she retrieved the call there was no one there. Whoever it was had not left a message. Kelly called the auto shop but there was no answer. She thought maybe Charlie might have tried to call her so she called his cell. He answered and said he hadn't called but he was fixing to call her. This was his weekend with his little boy Alex. His ex-wife was out of town.

He said Alex was having an asthma attack and that he had to stay with him and keep him home for the rest of his visit. That meant he wouldn't to be able to work on her car until Monday.

Kelly called and told Kim her situation. Kim was free that weekend because her ex-husband would be keeping their daughter so she told Kelly she could take her wherever she needed to go. They decided to make an afternoon of it and go to the mall. Kelly wanted to shop for a new purse. Kim picked her up around 1:00 PM. When they got to the mall they had some lunch and browsed in some of the stores. Kim dropped her off around 6:00 PM. It was dark by then. Kelly had forgotten to leave any lights on in the house. She said goodnight to Kim and got out of the car. As she approached the steps she had an odd feeling. She had gotten use to going in through the back alley entrance. Except for two corner street lights at the end of the street, the whole block of houses appeared in totally darkness.

She looked up at the large white columns on the house in all their magnificence. She still felt in awe at the beauty of the house and still couldn't get use to the fact that this was really her home now. The crystal glass in the front porch door sparkled in the distant street light. She carefully climbed the front stairs then leaped from the top step onto the porch. She looked both ways down each side of the porch. She could now hear her dogs barking inside the house. They must have been in the back of the house she thought and they must have heard the creaking of the old wooden front porch. As Kelly approached the door she could now hear them running and barking louder as they made a beeline to the front door.

Kelly unlocked the front door and stuck her arm inside and turned on the front porch light and the upstairs hall light to give the living room light as well. Her biggest dog Chloe barked the loudest when she came in and kept barking as though she didn't recognize her. She could hear the phone ringing as she opened the door. By the time she reached it, the caller had hung up. The caller ID display said unidentified number. This was the third call she had gotten like that since morning with an unidentified number and no message. She fed her dogs and let them out briefly. It had been a long day. She didn't like not having her car and she felt very tired and stressed. She took a shower and decided to go straight to bed.

CHAPTER 31

She turned all the lights off, checked the doors and retreated upstairs to her bedroom. She woke up around 12:00 pm. She sat up startled by the sound of loud dripping. Only this time it was louder than she had ever heard it before. The sounds seemed to resonate through the walls as Plop! Plop! Plop! The dripping sounds were traveling throughout the house. The dripping had a strange echo that seemed to give off a vibrating sound. The sound reminded Kelly of the sound of a bell in a tower except a bell sound in a well with an echo.

Kelly threw herself up in a sitting position. Her head was pounding. She turned the bedside light on and then jumped up and turned the bedroom overhead light on. The hall light was on. She placed her hands around her throat. "Why is the hall light on?" She asked herself. She remembered she had turned it off. She raced down the hall to the two bathrooms. Still half asleep she checked each one. The faucets were ok. They were not dripping or running. They were turned off. She stood in the hall listening. She thought "Oh God the dripping sound is back." "Let me think, let me think" she murmured. "It's the same dripping sound I heard before when I was convinced that it was coming from the attic, because I thought I had a leak in the attic or in the upstairs bedroom. But now, it sounds like it is coming from everywhere in the house."

Kelly was tired and dazed from being awakened in the middle of a sound sleep. She tried to remember again that the first time she heard the dripping was the day that she was in the upstairs bedroom. She had been certain that there was a leak and that the dripping sound was coming from there or in the attic. She remembered; "That day I looked around in the attic and the dripping stopped. That is all I remember, so what am I missing?" She tried to think. "Then the leak in the kitchen ceiling began dripping that awful stuff." "I wonder she said to herself, if the ceiling is dripping right now. The sound seems to be coming from the attic but then I hear it everywhere." She was terrified. She could hear her heart pounding in her chest. She thought she had better go downstairs and take a look. It wasn't until right then did she realize she had become deeply engulfed in paranormal experience. She could see that a light was on downstairs and knew it had to be the kitchen.

She locked her dogs in her room and then walked down the steps very cautiously. As she entered the kitchen she could see the basement door was cracked and the basement light was on. "Oh my God she thought" as she grabbed at the top of her gown. She walked very lightly to the basement door. She was afraid to open the door all the way and look down. Instead, she quickly shut it and shoved the latch closed to secure the lock in place. She knew she hadn't been down in the basement for at least a week. The basement door was closed when she came home or she would have noticed it. Someone was either already in the house when she came in or they broke in after she went to bed. Since her car wasn't there they thought she was gone. They could have entered the house through the front door or the back door, or even the basement. They must have heard me come in and left by the basement door.

Someone must have been looking for something in the basement. But Kelly knew she wasn't about to go down there then. "All I know she thought is, something has upset this house." That sounds strange to say but she felt like something in house had been disturbed. She checked all the rooms down stairs. The dripping sound continued and seemed to be loudest in the kitchen. "I need to get my gun" she thought and turned to go back upstairs. But she stopped when she suddenly heard footsteps and talking coming from upstairs. "It sounds like it's coming from the attic like before." She thought, as she returned to the kitchen.

Her attention was diverted to the dried brown circles on the ceiling above the sink. As she watched in horror they began turning blood red before her eyes. She thought she was hallucinating as she stood staring in horror as the circles grew larger and larger. Kelly stepped back to the kitchen door. Drops of gooey red liquid began dripping into the sink and on counter making an echoing sound with each drip, drip, plop, plop. She stood there speechless. The red liquid was splashing in the sink and splattering on the sides of the counter top. She screamed and ran to the sink and tried wiping it up with paper towels as it kept dripping. She turned and raced back upstairs but she didn't know where to go or what to do next. She could still hear the dripping sounds coming from above her head and echoing throughout the entire upstairs hallway. She couldn't escape the sounds in her bedroom. The walking sounds and the voices continued while the dripping sounds continued to echo throughout the entire house. She was beyond being terrified. She was shaking and trembling all over.

She grabbed her purse and her cell phone and ran down the stairs to leave the house. She thought I will call Kim and I will have to stay at her house tonight and then I am leaving this house for good tomorrow and I am never coming back. Suddenly the dripping sounds and the voices stopped. She stood very still for a few minutes to see what would happen next. She then sat down on the couch and pulled her ice cold feet up to her chest covering them with a pillow. She tried to think clearly. She got up and walked to the front door and looked out across the yard into the solid darkness. Her eyes were open wide searching desperately in the dark for something, anything, maybe the intruder. She wondered if whoever had broken in was scared away by the dripping noise and left by the basement door. She sat on the living room couch without any cover and with all the house lights on. The house remained quiet but she didn't sleep for the rest of the night. The next morning Kelly still had the mind set to leave the house but she wanted to get to the bottom of the break-in. She went outside to check the basement door. Since the door was only equipped with an outside lock her worst fear was answered. Just as she had surmised the outside basement door was open.

While Kelly was out Saturday the intruder probably came in through the basement door. That would explain why Chloe was barking so loudly when she came home. The intruder may have still been there at the time. He could have entered through the basement door and then left the same way. She found the basement door lock hanging on the outside of the door and she remembered she hadn't left it that way. Kelly walked inside the basement and looked around the way she thought that person would have done. There was nothing of any value down there, only some old tools, flower pots, and the washer and dryer. The rest were pictures, lamps and odds and ends that she had put there when she moved in until she decided on a place to put them. Nothing really looked disturbed except some boxes against the wall that had been pulled out and gone through and the doors on an old wooden cabinet that was there when she moved in were open. What could they have been looking for? She looked around again then walked outside and closed the outside door and secured it with the pad lock. She wondered "Could whoever broke in been scared away by the dripping sounds that woke me up?"

CHAPTER 32

Kelly thought that while she was investigating she would look up in the attic since she had heard the dripping again coming from there. To her wonder, the boxes that had been so neatly closed and stacked together on her last look up there were now open and the contents of clothes and books were pulled out on the floor. She figured that the same person must have ransacked the attic at the same time that they broke in through the basement while she was at the mall with Kim. But Kelly also figured that if someone had a door key, they could have come in at almost any time while she was away from home or at work to look up in the attic in search of whatever they were in search of. They were definitely looking for something she concluded. "It is strange" she thought "that they are just rummaging through things, not taking anything of any real value but just going through stuff like they are searching for something but what could they be looking for?" She also decided to get all the locks changes as soon as possible.

Kelly reported the break-in to the police. Then a week passed and two weeks passed and she had still not heard from Steve about the kitchen ceiling. She had decided to sell the house but was trying to make up her mind when to move out and where to move temporarily until she could buy her another home. She felt she had finally taken all she could. When she was at home she couldn't enjoy her home anymore. Most of the time she was totally consumed with the leak in the kitchen ceiling and the dripping sounds, the sounds coming from the attic and all of the other paranormal events that now were occurring. She could no longer deal with the insanity and was now questioning her own sanity.

From time to time she would walk into the kitchen and stare up at the ceiling at the large dried brown circles, just wondering when it would start dripping again. She had loved this house or had tried to love it. But she was at her wits end. It had been two weeks since the last incident and all was quiet but she knew things were still not normal. She wondered "will things ever be normal again?" She walked into the kitchen one afternoon after it had been raining and to her disbelief a large old brown circle was turning red again. Then from nowhere other circles began to form that began spreading on the ceiling filling with wet red liquid before her eyes.

She couldn't believe how huge the first one was becoming. It was brownish red and gooey looking and had spread to the outer corner of the ceiling and had begun to creep down the wall against the top of the window. It looked very macabre. The loud dripping returned as the spots grew and the sound of dripping began to echo through the house. Several watered down bloody looking circles had spread across the ceiling above the doorway and were dripping from the ceiling. Kelly gathered all the buckets she had and placed them under larger leaks until they could no longer catch the growing number of drips and splatters. She watched as a large drop hit the sink and spattered outward. She heard a crackling noise and glanced at the wall as a slow moving stream of brown goo gushed from the old wallpaper down the wall into a red pool in the floor by the back door. The dripping sound echoed throughout the house each time a drop would hit the bucket she had placed under it. She couldn't handle the drama any longer and that day moved to a motel room. When she returned in two days all was quiet again and the circles were beginning to dry up.

At that point Kelly became very agitated and picked up the phone and called Bill Saunders. Hi, this is Kelly Brown. Your worker Steve told me three weeks ago he would be back out here to tear out the kitchen ceiling to see why it's leaking or go up on the roof to see if he could find where the leak was coming from, but he still hasn't called or come by, and now it is twice as bad. It's dripping in the floor. It looks really nasty it's rusty red water. I've got buckets sitting all over the place. "I have tried to be patient Mr. Saunders said Kelly, but ya'll have given me really bad service." Mr. Saunders apologized and said that they'd be out there the next day at 8:00 am.

CHAPTER 33

That night Kelly fell asleep on the couch watching the late show. She woke up around 2:00 AM with a horrible migraine. She had been dreaming. As she walked to the bathroom to get her migraine prescription, she began remembering her dream. She was up in the attic. The attic window seemed larger than before. The window was open all the way. There was a cool breeze blowing through it as she stood at the window looking out. Suddenly she saw Joe Hardy standing in the yard beside the myrtle tree. His face was tan and warm in appearance not cold and grey looking. His eyes sparkled like a blue sky. His arms were lifted high up in the air. He was looking up towards the back yard roof. That's all she could remember of her dream. She went upstairs and went to bed for the rest of the night.

The next morning Kelly tried to remember more of her dream as she drank a cup of coffee and waited for Saunders and Steve. Finally around 9:00 AM they drove into the back yard driveway. Kelly could see a tall extension ladder on the back of their truck. "Finally, maybe now" she thought "they will get something done." She stood by the window and waited for them to get to the back door before she opened it and greeted them. Bill Saunders with his usual unexpressive face came in and asked to look at the leak on the ceiling from the inside again. She took him to the kitchen. Steve who followed behind Saunders smiled and nodded at Kelly as he walked passed her. They all three starred up at the large wet red-brown circles that were positioned all over the ceiling. Steve said "I haven't looked at the roof yet, so I'd like to do that before I tare open the ceiling just to rule out any problem up there." He looked at Kelly and smiled and said "I'll go to the attic and go out that window and take a look around to see if I can pin point any problem." He turned and headed for the stairs. They heard him pull the ladder down and in a moment he was walking above their heads and talking to himself.

"Sorry we were late little lady" said Mr. Saunders. "I told Steve we had to be here at 8:00." He continued as he walked around in circles while glancing up at the ceiling, "Well, I guess I shouldn't be so hard on him. He's trying to do better and right now he's all I got." "Is something wrong" asked Kelly? "Oh, my nephew, he's really smart. He can be a good worker when he wants to be. He was late coming in again today. It's always the same thing. It's this way every Monday. I've told him for years that I'd fire him if he didn't quit laying out drunk and messing up my roofing jobs." "You mean Steve is your nephew?" asked Kelly. "Yeah, you didn't know that?" said Saunders. "No sir, I sure didn't" said Kelly. "Well, you see I've had to rely on him since I hurt my leg on a job from a fall some years back. Joe was hoping me for awhile but of course now he's gone. I can't climb roofs anymore so I rely on Steve to help me out." "Oh, so you didn't help Joe Hardy put the roof on this house?" asked Kelly. "No mam" replied Mr. Saunders "it wasn't me." "I came with Steve that day in the truck but he and Joseph put the roof on until well, till Joseph fell and you know how that ended. I only helped out some with the equipment."

Kelly thought back at her conversation with Mr. Westbrook about Mr. Saunders. He had mentioned Mr. Saunders's nephew to her. Steve was the nephew! Mr. Westbrook said Saunders's nephew took him for granted. He said he had a spiteful nephew who drank and laid off from work half the time but thought his uncle's business would one day be his until Joe started working for him. Mr. Westbrook said that Bill said Joe was a real go-getter and was giving him all the better paying jobs because his nephew laid off drunk all the time. Kelly just couldn't believe it. Steve was Mr. Saunders's nephew.

"Well," said Saunders, "I'm gona run out to the truck and try pulling the ladder off." Mr. Saunders turned and walked out the back door. Kelly stood in the kitchen thinking to herself. She thought she would go out back and watch Steve working on the roof so she walked out the back door into the yard and glanced up at the roof while shielding the sun from her eyes with her hand. Steve was standing on the right side of the house with one foot position on the edge of the roof. He yelled down at them. "I think I see where the problem is but I can't get up under these tiles with this hammer." Saunders began pulling out different tools from the back of the truck. "Steve, I've got something you can use yelled Kelly. I'll be right up." Kelly hurried in the back door and grabbed the crow bar from under the sink. She was still pondering as to why he had lied to her about not being on the roof the day of Joe's accident.

Kelly climbed the attic stairs and boosted herself up onto the attic floor. As she approached the attic window where she first retrieved the crowbar the truth suddenly came to her. Steve was standing outside the window wiping the sweat from his forehead with the bottom of his shirt. "Here you go," said Kelly in a hurried voice. "Maybe this will work." Steve turned to see her leaning out the window and he smiled. She smiled back. Then he saw the crowbar in her hand. He starred at it for a moment then he looked at her. She could see a sudden look of fear in his eyes as he took the crowbar from her hand. At first he hesitated to take it. He blinked his eyes several times and then carefully took it out of her hand. He took a deep breath as he examined it, turning it over and over until he found what he was looking for, the blood stain. She heard him breathe a sigh of relief. "Thanks, he said. This should do it." She was now looking directly at him but he wouldn't look her in the eyes. She spoke up and said; "I'm glad it'll work." As she turned to go back down the stairs he yelled at her "Hey, Kelly! Can we talk later?" "I've had something on my mind I want to talk to you about." Kelly said "Sure ok, later." She smiled at him and climbed down the stairs and hurried out the back door into the yard where Saunders was waiting at his truck.

CHAPTER 34

Kelly stood outside with Saunders. They both watched Steve as he returned to the end of the roof and began to pry up the shingles with the crowbar. "The sun must be playing tricks on my eyes, thought Kelly. I can't believe what I'm seeing." It was Joe standing on the roof in front of Steve. Steve was bent down on one knee working with the crowbar prying up a shingle when all of a sudden he stopped and looked up. He must have seen Joe's work boots because he looked up and then slowly rose to a standing position never taking his eyes off of Joe. They stood face to face. Then Steve yelled "no!" and began to walk backwards. Mr. Saunders yelled "watch it boy you're fixin to fall!" Steve took another step backwards. The heel of his boot lodged on the corner of the roof as he flung his arms trying to regain his balance. The crowbar flew from his hand as he fell backwards to the ground. Kelly screamed, "Oh my God" as she ran to Steve. Mr. Saunders ran to the side of the house yelling Steve's name over and over again. Steve never answered. It appeared he must have died instantly from the fall. The coroner's exam concluded he died of a broken neck. Kelly was traumatized for weeks and attended several therapy sessions compounded with a lot of praying & meditating to deal with anxiety and reoccurring dreams.

Kelly was now certain that Joe died not because of the jealousy Bill Saunders had for Joe but because of the jealousy Steve had for Joe. Steve had murdered Joe with the crowbar. Their voices were the voices she had heard coming from the attic that were projected by Joe. They had argued in the attic the day of his death. That explained the footsteps she heard. They had fought the day Joe died. The crowbar had been the murder weapon and Steve had killed him with the crowbar and pushed him off the roof. He must have dropped the crowbar after he hit Joe and didn't see where it fell beneath the window and lay wedged between the wooden floor boards where it stayed until Kelly found it.

Joe's blood is on the crowbar and Steve's fingerprints. Kelly realized it all now and wondered in amazement could Joe have actually laid a plan of revenge for the man who murdered him by using Kelly's psychic abilities to carry out his plan by drawing her to the house through dreams? Steve must have felt a heavy guilt and was drawn to the house in search of the murder weapon. Steve was the man in the alley. He was the one who broke into her house and ransacked the basement and the attic searching for the murder weapon. Steve was use to controlling people, always getting what he wanted. He must have felt his future as owner of his uncle's business was being jeopardized by Joe so he had to get him out of the way, but by killing Joe he also jeopardized his freedom. It appears that in the end Joe got his revenge.

The day Steve died Kelly needed to pray and meditate. She walked through the small white room and stopped at the doorway entrance. Directly in front of her was nothing but a total dark void. She barely glanced to the right because she knew there wasn't anything but darkness. Instead she looked to the left and to the door with the small window at the top where a ray of light streamed through. She opened the door to see a beautiful garden. She could sense the stone floor was warm from the shining sun. There were green vines and flowering plants that hung on the wall of the garden to the left. She started to enter when she sensed the presence of someone behind her. She looked back over her shoulder. Although she could not see who was there she felt there was not one but two who followed behind her.

She welcomed them and they followed her as she proceeded to the left down the stone trail to the garden room entrance. There she stopped and motioned with her hand. The two of them entered the garden area together. This time she did not go in. She left them there knowing they were now where they needed to be. Their search for peace had come at last. When Kelly awoke she felt a new sense of purpose in her life again. Why had she meditated this and who were these two that had followed her into herself proclaimed sanctuary? Kelly knew in her heart there was one soul that she hoped would now be laid to rest and there was another who was there she hoped to also seek forgiveness. She prayed they would both find peace.

CHAPTER 35

I t was now April. It had rained off and on it seemed every other day. In the weeks that followed nature was gradually taking hold as everything in sight began to bloom. The grass and plants surrounding the house began coming out of its metamorphosis. Kelly remembered back to when she bought the house and how it had gone from a beautiful home in a picture Mrs. Westbrook had shown her to a home that Kelly had fallen in love with but then struggled to be happy in with all she had been through from the dreams about the house, the haunting of Joe, and meeting Steve. Joe's revenge had traumatized her as well as the death of Steve. She had struggled so hard emotionally in search of the truth about Joe Hardy's death, not to mention after awhile even questioning her own sanity.

It had been only six months since she moved into the house. The dream about the house no longer haunted Kelly. The mystery surrounding Joe Hardy's death had been solved. The circles on the kitchen ceiling had completely disappeared and things were now as clear as this sunny morning. She believed that now her life would be better because she had a new purpose in life full of new dreams. She would never fight her insightful gifts again but would learn to embrace them with true conviction. Kelly was full of hope and she knew she would finally be content in her home. Past problems that were once sealed in the walls had been resolved. It will now be a happier place to live.

CHAPTER 36

Kelly had never noticed how in the mornings the sunlight streamed in every room that faced the back yard. She was in the kitchen one morning preparing breakfast when she felt a cool breeze behind her. She turned around and there was Joe. He was almost transparent whereas before his presence had been totally visual in appearance. He stood there staring straight ahead with those searching eyes. She could almost see the cabinets thru him. He starred at her for a moment. He had a content look on his face. The sadness was gone. As Kelly looked on his image it began to fade until he disappeared. She looked out the window remembering the first time she saw him in the back yard, standing by the myrtle tree. Now shinning on that tree was a bright light. She walked outside to witness the most beautiful rainbow she had ever seen. Actually the only one she had ever seen that close. The colors were so bright and vivid they seemed to pop out. It shown there like a crescent water fall streaming in perpetual motion as the array of colors glistened in the air over the wet morning rain. Kelly smiled as she followed its path up and up as far as she could see as it stretched for miles and miles into the sky until it was gone. Wow, she thought this is either the beginning of the rainbow or the end of it. She decided that it had to be a sign from Joe that it was a new beginning.

Kelly still lives in her beautiful southern mansion home and has grown to love it well. Steve's death surrounded her with some inquisitive publicity for awhile. Kelly will never know what Steve wanted to talk to her about. Whatever it was, she liked to believe that he was really remorseful for what he had done and that's what he wanted to discuss with her. Whenever she is asked about his death she says he is someone she cared for but only knew for a short time. And as for Joe, if anyone ever asked her what she knew about him, she would just say she heard he was a good guy in the prime of this life who didn't deserve to die so young.

The End